Research Collections In Microform In Ontario and Quebec University Libraries

Compiled By
Iqbal Wagle
University of Toronto Library

Ontario Council of University Libraries
Conférence des Recteurs et des Principaux des Universités du Québec
1979

The cover photograph is of an early microfilm reader: "The Optigraph Reading Machine." Manufactured in the U.S.A. about 1937 by the International Filmbook Corporation, this model is still in working order.

The text of this publication was prepared at the University of Toronto Library for printing and distribution by:

McMaster University Library Press,
Mills Memorial Library,
McMaster University,
1280 Main Street West,
Hamilton, Ontario, Canada.
L8S 4L6

© 1979 Ontario Council of University Libraries,
Conférence des Recteurs et des
Principaux des Universités du Québec

I.S.B.N. 0-919592-04-X

CONTENTS

Introduction   v

Location Symbols vii

Abbreviations   ix

Alphabetical List of Research Collections in Microform . . 1-106

Author/Title Index 107-143

INTRODUCTION

The first <u>Union List of Microform Sets in O.C.U.L. Libraries</u> was published in 1961 with 97 entries. The present one lists major collections in microform housed in Ontario and Quebec university libraries, with 634 entries. It does not however include monographs or individual serial titles such as newspapers and journals. The criterion of selection for inclusion has been the research value of the collections and their usefulness to University researchers. There is an extensive author/title index.

Accessibility to any one collection is often improved by a guide and such guides, when they could be located, have been cited following the individual entries. The guides generally offer bibliographic information relating to individual microform collections. They may also refer to the bibliographies from which the publishers have reproduced all or some titles in microform.

I would like to express my thanks to the contributing libraries; without their active co-operation a project of this nature would not have been feasible. My thanks are also due to Mrs. Rosy Akonteh for promptly and efficiently typing the preliminary and the final draft and to Mrs. Gloria Williams for typing the Index.

                                          Iqbal Wagle
                                          University of Toronto Library

LOCATION SYMBOLS

OGU	University of Guelph, Guelph
OHM	McMaster University, Hamilton
OKQ	Queen's University, Kingston
OLU	University of Western Ontario, London
OOCC	Carleton University, Ottawa
OOU	University of Ottawa
OPAL	Lakehead University, Thunder Bay
OPET	Trent University, Peterborough
OSTCB	Brock University, St. Catharines
OSUL	Laurentian University, Sudbury
OTR	Ryerson Polytechnical Institute, Toronto
OTU	University of Toronto, Toronto
OTY	York University, Toronto
OTYL	Law Library, York University, Toronto
OWA	University of Windsor, Windsor
OWL	Wilfrid Laurier University, Waterloo
OWTU	University of Waterloo, Waterloo
QLB	Bishop's University, Lennoxville
QMG	Sir George Williams Campus, Concordia University, Montréal
QMM	McGill University, Montréal
QMML	Law Library, McGill University, Montréal
QQLA	Université Laval, Québec
QRUQR	Centre d'études Universitaires dans l'Ouest Québécois, Québec
QSHERU	Université de Sherbrooke

ABBREVIATIONS

(L) Available on Interlibrary Loan*

(P) Will provide Photocopy

Mcd   Microcard

Mfe   Microfiche

Mfm   Microfilm

Mpt   Microprint

*Interlibrary Loan:

Most libraries lend microforms on Interlibrary Loan although some restrict them to library use only, especially when government documents and other heavily used items are involved. The University of Guelph (OGU) and York University (OTY) do not have "L" or "P" included with their respective locations, because the former deals with Interlibrary Loan requests on an individual basis and will lend material if items are not in heavy use, while the latter provides printed copy from all microforms and lends the microforms themselves only with very few exceptions.

9. Allied Powers Reparation Commission. <u>Reparation Papers of the Allied Powers Reparation Commission, 1922-1930</u>. Arlington, Va., University, 1975. 6 reels.

    OHM mfm (LP)
    OSUL mfm (LP)
    OWL mfm (LP)
    OWTU mfm (LP)

10. <u>Almanach National; Annuaire Officiel de la Republique Francaise, 1770-1879</u>. Microcard Editions, Washington, D.C., 1966.

    OLU mfe (LP)

11. <u>American Colonial Records; Records for the 18th and 19th Centuries in 15 Eastern States</u>. New Haven, Conn., Research Publications, 1970. 168 reels.

    OKQ mfm (L)
    OOU mfm (L)
    QMG mfm (L)

12. <u>American Culture Series, 1493-1806</u>. Ann Arbor, Mich., University Microfilms, 1941. 26 reels.

    OWA mfm (LP)

    Guide: <u>Bibliography of American Culture 1439-1875</u>. Compiled and edited by David R. Weimer, Ann Arbor, Mich., University Microfilms, 1957.

13. <u>American Fiction</u>. Ser.1: 1774-1850; ser.2: 1851-1875; ser.3: 1876-1900. Louisville, Ky. Lost Cause Press. New Haven, Conn., Research Publications. In progress.

    OGU mcd ser.1-2   OWA mfm ser.1-2 (LP)
    OLU mfm ser.1-3 (LP) OWTU mfm ser.1 and Supplement (LP)
    OOCC mfm ser.1-2 (LP)

    Guides: <u>American Prose Fiction 1774-1900 Cumulative Author Index</u>. Ann Arbor, Mich., Xerox University Microfilms, 1974.

        Wright, L.H. <u>American Fiction, 1851-1875</u>. San Marino, Calif., Huntington Library, 1965.

        Wright, Lyle H. <u>American Fiction, 1774-1850</u>. San Marino, Calif., Huntington Library Publications 2nd Edition, 1948.

        Wright, Lyle H. <u>American Fiction, 1876-1900</u>. San Marino, Calif., Huntington Library, 1966.

14. American Literature of the 19th Century. Ser. A: Ohio Valley., Ser. B: The South., Ser. C: Trans-Missippippi West. Louisville, Lost Cause Press.

    OGU mcd ser. A,B,C.   OWA m d ser. A   (L)
    OHM mcd ser. A (LP)

15. American Periodical Series I, 1741-1800. Ann Arbor, Mich., University Microfilms. 1942?

    OLU mfm (LP)   QMG mfm   (L)

    Guide: Early American Periodicals Index, 1728-1850. New York, Readex Microprint Corp., 1964.

16. American Periodical Series II, 1800-1850. Ann Arbor, Mich., University Microfilms, 1942.

    OLU mfm (LP)
    QMG mfm (L)

    Guide: American Periodicals Series: A Consolidated Index to the Microfilm Series of the 18th Century Periodicals and to the First 10 Years of the 1800-1850 Series, Ann Arbor, Mich., University Microfilms, 1956.

17. Archiv Kniaziâ Voront'sova Moscow, 1870-1895. Tumba, Sweden, International Documentation Centre. 452 fiche.

    QMM mfe (P)

18. Archives de la Linguistique Francaise; Collection de Documents Relatifs a la Langue Francaise, Publiees Entre 1500 et 1900. Paris, France-Expansion, 1972-

    OHM mfe (incomplete holdings) (LP)   OTU mfe (LP)
    OOU mfe (lacking some titles) (LP)

19. Archives de la Rochelle (France) S.L. Archives Départementales de la Charente-Maritime. Montreal, Universite McGill, 1966. 4 reels.

    QSHERU mfm (L)

20. Archives Diplomatiques, Correspondance Consulaire D'Odessa. Odessa, Ministere des Affaires Etrangeres, 1802-20. Paris, Service International de Microfilms, S.D. Reel 1.

    QSHERU mfm (L)

21. Archives Diplomatiques; Recueil Mensuel de Diplomatic D'Histoire et de Droit International. Washington, D.C., Microcard Editions Inc., 1967.

    OTU mfe (Ser.1, 1861-79)
              (Ser.2, 1880-1900)
              (Ser.3, 1901-13)
              (Ser.4, 1914) (LP)

22. Archives Parlementaires de 1787 a 1860: Recueil Complet des Debats Legislatifs & Politiques de Chambres Francaises. 1st Ser. v.1-82, 1787-1799, 2d Ser. v.1-106, 1800-1860. Washington: NCR Microcard Editions, 1967- .

    OGU   mfe
    OKQ   mfe (Ser.1, 1787-1793/4, Ser.2, 1814-1839) (LP)
    OOCC mfe (P)
    OOU   mfe (LP)

23. Art Exhibition Catalogues Republished on Microfiche. Cambridge, Eng., Chadwyck, 1975.

    OOCC mfe (P)

24. Association of Research Libraries. Center for Chinese Research Materials. Chinese Maritime Customs Publications Chung-Kuo Hai-Kuan Ch'u-Pan P'in 1860-1948. Boston, Harvard University Library Micro Reproduction Service, 1970. 100 reels.

    QMM mfm (P)

25. Association Universitaire Pour la Diffusion Internationale de la Recherche. Bibliotheque de Recherche. Etudes de Sinologie. Paris: AUDIR-Hachette/ Bibliotheque Nationale; New York: Clearwater Pub. Co., 1976. 31 fiche.

    OKQ   mfe (LP)
    OWTU mfe (LP)

26. Australia. Royal Commission on Australian Government Administration. Collected Papers of the Royal Commission on Australian Government Administration, 1974. Canberra, Australian Govt. Pub. Service, 1977.

    OKQ mfe (LP)

27. Berlin (West Berlin) Allied Kommandatura. <u>Official Gazette of the Allied Kommandatura Berlin.</u> Amtsblatt der Alliierten Kommandatura Berlin 1950-1965. N.Y., Millwood, KTO Microform, Rte.

    OWTU   mfm   (LP)

28. Bible. N.T. Gospels. Greek. <u>Gospels in Greek 11th Century.</u> East Ardsley, Yorkshire, Micro Methods Ltd. 1 reel.

    OTR   mfm   (L)

29. Bible. O.T. Pentateuch. Judeo-Persian. 1973. <u>Biblia Judaeo-Persica/</u> Herbert H. Paper. -- Editio Variorum. Ann Arbor, Mich. University Microfilms 1973. 5 reels.
    The texts represented include manuscripts (the earliest dated 1319 A.D.) from a variety of collections in London, New York, Cincinnati, and Rome, in addition to the texts of two printed versions (Constantinople 1546 and Jerusalem 1904)

    OTU   mfm   (LP)

30. Boccaccio, Giovanni. <u>Decameron.</u> East Ardsley, Eng., Micro Methods Ltd. 1 reel.

    OTR   mfm   (L)

31. <u>Books Printed in the Netherlands and Belgium Before 1601.</u> Lexington, Ky. Erasmus Press, 1967-   ; Cambridge, Mass., Microfilm Editions, 1967-

    OGU   mfm   (reels 1-42)

    Guide: British Museum. Dept. of Printed Books. <u>Short-Title Catalogue of Books Printed in the Netherlands and Belgium and of Dutch and Flemish Books......</u> 1470-1600 Now in the British Museum. London, 1965.

32. Borden, (Sir) Robert Laird. <u>The Borden Papers, 1893-1937,</u> Ottawa Public Archives of Canada, 1952-

    OTU   mfm   (LP)

33. Borden, (Sir) Robert Laird. <u>Diary of Sir Robert Borden: Washington Disarmament Conference 1921-1922.</u> Ottawa, Public Archives of Canada, 1952-

    OTU   mfm   (LP)

34. Boucher, Pierre. Fonds Boucher. Seigneurie Boucherville a Concessions 1716-20. Registre des Baptêmes et Sepultures á Faits Aux Trois-Rivieres, s.d. Montréal, Société Canadienne de Microfilm, 1970.

    QSHERU mfm (L)

35. Bourassa, Henri. Articles de Henri Bourassa Publiés dans le Devoir. v.1-10; 1910-1932. Montréal, Recordak.

    OSUL mfm (LP)   QSHERU mfm (L)
    OTU   mfm (LP)

36. Bourassa, Henri. Papiers de Henri Bourassa et Sa Correspondance. Ottawa, Archives Publiques du Canada, 1967. 2 reels.

    OSUL mfm (LP)   OWA mfm (LP)

    Guide: Gergevin, André. Henri Bourassa (par) André Bergeron, Cameron Nish et Anne Bourassa. Montréal, Editions de L'Action Nationale, 1966.

37. Britain and Europe Since 1945. Brighton, Eng., Harvester Press, 1973-

    OHM mfe (LP)   OWTU mfe (1973-1976) (LP)
    OOCC mfe

38. British and Continental Rhetoric and Elocution. Collection of 200 Texts on Rhetorical and Elocutionary Theory. v.p., 1520-1826. Ann Arbor, Mich., University Microfilms, 1969. 143v. in 149. 16 reels.

    OTU   mfm (LP)   QMM mfm (P)
    OWTU mfm

    Guide: University Microfilms, Ann Arbor, Mich., British and Continental Rhetoric and Elocution. Ann Arbor, Mich., University Microfilms, 1969?

39. British Birth Control Material at the British Library of Political and Economic Sciences, 1800-1947. London, Eng., World Microfilms Publications Ltd., 1972. 10 reels.

    OLU mfm (LP
    QMM mfm

40. British Cabinet Papers on Microfilm, 1902-1945. London, Public Record Office.

    OLU   mfm   (LP)

41. British Columbia. British Columbia Gazette, 1957-   N.Y., Recordak Corp.

    OTU   mfm   (P)

42. British Columbia. Laws, Statutes, etc. Revised Statutes, 1871-1897. Ottawa, Canadian Library Association.

    OGU   mfm   1871-1897

43. British Columbia. Legislative Assembly. Journals, 1872-1903. Ottawa, Canadian Library Association.

    OGU   mfm   (1872-1903)   OTU   mfm   (1871-1900)

44. British Columbia. Legislative Assembly. Sessional Papers, 1876-1903. Ottawa, Canadian Library Association.

    OGU   mfm   (1876-1903)   OTY   mfm   (1876-1902)

45. British Conservative Party. Archives of the British Conservative Party. Pamphlets and Leaflets, Ser.1, 1868-1914. Hassocks, London, Eng., Harvester Press.

    OHM   mfe   (LP)

46. British Culture Series; a Selection of Books Relationg to English Culture of the 18th and 19th Centuries. Louisville, Lost Cause Press.

    OGU   mcd   OWTU   mcd   (L)

47. British Labour History Ephemera. Pamphlets, 1-1159, 1900-1926. London, Eng. World Microfilm Publications, 1973. 22 reels.

    OLU   mfm   (1900-1926)   (LP)   OWA   mfm   (LP)

48. British Labour Party. Archives of the British Labour Party. Pamphlets and Leaflets, ser.1, 1900-1959, ser.2, 1900-1926. Hassocks, London, Eng., Harvester Press.

    OHM   mfe   (LP)

49. British Records Relating to America in Microform. East Ardsley, Yorks;
    Micro Methods, 1964-   .

    OHM   mfm   (LP)
    OOU   mfm   (LP)   Titles Separately Catalogued
    OTU   mfm   (LP)   Titles Separately Catalogued
    QMG   mfm   (L)

    Guides: British Records Relating to America in Microform. 2d ed. East
            Ardsley, England: EP Microform, n.d. lists items included in
            the collection, gives brief annotations, numbers of reels,
            prices, etc.
            Crick, Bernard Rowland and Alman, Miriam, eds. A Guide to
            Manuscripts Relating to America in Great Britain and Ireland.
            Westport: Published for the British Association for American
            Studies by Meckler Books, 1978.

50. British Trade Union History Collection: Major Works on the Trade Unions
    and Their Leaders from Their Inception to the Present Day, v.p., 1831-
    1971. London, World Microfilms, c1974. 49 reels.

    OWA   mfm   (LP)
    QMM   mfm   (P)

51. Buchez, Phillippe J. Histoire Parlementaire de la Révolution Française,
    où Journal des Assemblés Nationales Depuis 1789 Jusqu'en 1815, 40v.
    1834-38. Washington, D.C., Microcard Editions.

    OOU   mfe   (LP)

52. Burghley, William Cecil, Baron. Politics and Administration of Tudor
    England: Lord Burghley's Papers in the British Library in London. --
    Hassocks, Eng.: Harvester Press, 1976. 43 reels.
    "Produced in its entirety from the Lansdowne Collection; edited by
    Michael Hawkins."

    OHM   mfm   (LP)

53. CAN/FIL; Canadian Financial Information Library. (Company Reports)
    Toronto, Bell and Howell, 1975-   .

    OWL   mfe   (LP)   QMG   mfe   (Selected Companies)   (L)

54. CANEDEX. Canadian Education Monographs on Microfiche. Webster, N.Y.:
    Photographic Services Corporation, 1974.

    OWTU   mfe   (#74.0001-74.131., 75.1-75.51)   (L)

55. California. Governor's Commission on the Los Angeles Riots. Transcripts Depositions, Consultant's Reports, and Selected Documents. 1965. Washington, D.C. Filmed by the Library of Congress Photoduplication Service for Microcard Editions, 1969? 5 reels.

    OKQ mfm (LP)   OWA mfm (LP)
    OTU mfm (LP)

56. Calvin, John. Opera Quae Supersunt Omnia, 1863-1900. 59v. in 26. Washington; Microcard Editions, 1965. 800 cards.

    OGU mcd

57. Camden Society London. Publications. Ser.1, v.1-105, 1838-1872. Washington, Microcard Editions.

    OSUL mfe (L)

    Guide: Nichols, John Gough. A Descriptive Catalogue of the First Series of the Works of the Camden Society 1806-1873. Accompanied by a Classified Arrangement and Index. 2d ed. Westminister, J.B. Nicholls & Sons, 1872.

58. Camden Society London. Publications. New Series v.1-62; 1871-1901. Washington, Microcard Editions.

    OSUL mfe (LP)

59. Canada. Census. Census of Canada, 1971, Maps in Enumeration Area Series. Ottawa, Public Archives of Canada. 113 reels.

    OKQ mfm (LP)   OTY mfm

60. Canada. Census. Census Returns. Ottawa, Public Archives.

OGU	mfm	Ontario, 1842-71
OHM	mfm	Canada West 1842-71 Manitoba: 1870, N.B.: 1851-71, N.S.: 1871. Quebec: 1825-71 (P)
OKQ	mfm	Ontario, 1842, 1851, 1861, 1871, Quebec, 1825, 1831, 1842, 1861, 1871, N.S., 1871 (L)
OLU	mfm	Canada West 1842, 1851, 1861, 1870-71 (LP)
OOCC	mfe	Complete set, 1851-1871 (P)
OSTCB	mfm	Canada West 1842, 1861 (LP)
OTY	mfm	Canada West 1842-1871 (L)

60. (Cont'd)

    OWL   mfm Ontario, 1842-1871 (L)
    OWTU mfe Complete set 1851-1871
    QLB   mfm Quebec, 1825, 1831, 1842, Quebec. Eastern Townships & Vicinity. 1851, 1861, 1871. (LP)
    QMG   mfm Ontario 1842-71, Quebec 1825-71, N.B. 1851-71, N.S. 1871, P.E.I. 1841, 1860-1 (L)
    QMM   mfm Quebec, 1825-71 (P)
    QSHERU mfm Quebec, 1825, 1831, 1842, 1851, 1861, 1871. (L)

61. Canada. Department of Indian Affairs. **Annual Report, 1880-1936**. Ottawa, Public Archives of Canada.

    OGU mfm

62. Canada. Department of Indian Affairs and Northern Development. **National Parks Bibliographies**. Ottawa, Public Archives. 1971

    OOU mfe (LP)   OSUL mfe (LP)

63. Canada. Federal Provincial Conferences. **Documents from Federal Provincial Conferences in Canada, 1887-1976**. Toronto, Micromedia, 1977.

    OSTCB mfe (LP)   OGU mfe

    Guide: Guide to Microfiche Edition by James Quantrell.

64. Canada. Parliament. House of Commons. **Canadian Parliamentary Proceedings and Sessional Papers, 1841-1970**. Washington, D.C., United States Historical Documents Institute.

    OPET mfm (1841-1925) (L)   OWL mfm (1841-1866) (L)
    OTU   mfm (1841-1866)

65. Canada. Parliament. House of Commons. **Debates** (Reported in Newspapers), **1846-1874**. Ottawa, Canadian Library Association, 5 reels.

    OGU   mfm (1858-1862, 1866-1870, 1873-1899)
    OPAL mfm (1846-1874) (LP)
    OPET mfm (1846-70, 1873-74) (LP)
    OSUL mfm (LP)
    OWTU mfm
    QMM   mfm (1866-1870, 1873-1874) (LP)
    QMML mfm (1846-1874) (LP)
    QQLA mfm (LP)

66. Canada. Parliament. House of Commons. Journals, 1867-1970. Washington, United States Historical Institute, Inc.

    OOCC   mfm   (P)

    Guide: Canada. Parliament. House of Commons. General Index to the House of Commons, 1867-1930. Ottawa, 1880-1932.

67. Canada. Parliament. House of Commons. Sessional Papers of the Dominion of Canada, 1867-1925. Washington, D.C., United States Historical Documents Institute. 317 reels.

    OGU   mfm   OTY   mfm
    OPAL   mfm   (1916-1923)   51 reels   (LP)   QMM   mfm   (1891-1910)
    OPET   mfm   (L)

68. Canada. Parliament. House of Commons. Unpublished Sessional Papers, 1916-1958. Ottawa: Public Archives.

    OGU   mfm   (1916-1939)   OSUL   mfm   (1916-1924)   (P)
    OHM   mfm   (1916-1924)   (L)   OTU   mfm
    OKQ   mfm   (1916-1923)   OWTU   mfm   (1916-1923)
    OLU   mfm   (1916-1924)   (LP)   QMG   mfm   (reels 1-15)   (L)
    OPAL   mfm   (1916-1923)   (LP)   QMM   mfm   (1916-1958)   (P)

69. Canada. Parliament. House of Commons. Standing and Special Committees. Reports and Minutes of Proceedings and Evidence, 1935-1970. Toronto, Micromedia, Ltd.

    OOCC   mfe
    OOU   mfe   (LP)

70. Canada. Parliament. Library. English Language Card Catalogue, 1976- Ottawa: Historical Documents Institute, 1975-

    OLU   mfm   (LP)   OTU   mfm

71. Canada. Parliament. Senate. Special Committee on Mass Media. Briefs, 1970. Toronto, Micromedia Ltd. 1975. 3 reels.

    OKQ   mfm   (LP)

    Guide: Loose leaf author index. List of briefs appears at the beginning of the film.

72. Canada. Public Archives. <u>Archives Canada Microfiches</u>. Ottawa, Information Canada, 1976-

    OKQ mfm (LP)

73. Canada. Public Archives. <u>Centennial Issues of Canadian Newspapers</u>. Ottawa. Public Archives of Canada, Microfilm Unit, 1969. 8 reels. (With Index)

    OKQ mfm (LP)
    OTU mfm (LP)

74. Canada. Public Archives. <u>Pamphlets in the Public Archives, 1493-1877</u>. Ottawa, Public Archives, 1969-

OGU	mfe		OWTU mfe	(Ser.1, no.322-1303 & ser.2) (LP)
OHM	mfe	(L)		
OOCC	mfe	(L)	QMG mfe	(1-1541) (L)
OPET	mfe	(L)	QMM mfe	(P)
OSTCB	mfe	(P)		
OSUL	mfe	(P)		
OTU	mfe	(P)		
OTY	mfe			

    Guide: Canada. Public Archives. <u>Catalogue of Pamphlets in the Public Archives of Canada Prepared by Magdalon Casey</u>. Ottawa, King's Printer, 1931-32, 2v.

75. Canada. Royal Commission of Inquiry into the Non-Medical use of Drugs, 1972. <u>Briefs and Transcripts</u>. Toronto, Micromedia.

    OOCC mfm (P)   OSTCB mfm (LP)
    OOU   mfm (LP)   OTY   mfm
    OPET mfm (L)

    Guide: Canada. Commission of Inquiry into the Non-Medical use of Drugs. <u>Index to Briefs and Transcripts of Hearings</u>. Toronto, Micromedia Ltd., 1973.

76. Canada. Royal Commission of Enquiry into the Non-Medical use of Drugs. <u>Research Papers</u>. Ottawa, Public Archives of Canada, 1974. 14 reels.

    OKQ   mfm (LP)   OOU   mfm (LP)
    OOCC mfm (P).   OSTCB mfm (LP)

77. Canada. Royal Commission on Bilingualism and Biculturalism. <u>Briefs and Transcripts, 1972</u>. Toronto, Micromedia, Ltd., 1972. 6 reels.

    OOCC mfm (P)   OTY mfm
    OOU   mfm (LP)

    Guide: Canada. Royal Commission on Bilingualism and Biculturalism. <u>Index to Briefs and Transcripts of Public Hearings</u>. Toronto, Micromedia Ltd., 1972.

78. Canada. Royal Commission on Bilingualism and Biculturalism. <u>Research Studies</u>. Ottawa, Canadian Library Association, 1970. Microfilm.

    OOCC mfm (P)   OTY mfm
    OOU   mfm (LP)
    OPET mfm (L)
    OSUL mfm (LP)

79. Canada. Royal Commission on Broadcasting, 1956. <u>Briefs and Transcripts</u>. Ottawa, Public Archives, 1974. 9 reels.

    OOU mfm (LP)

80. Canada. Royal Commission on Canada's Economic Prospects, 1955-1957. <u>Briefs and Transcripts</u>. Toronto, Micromedia Ltd. 1972. 25 reels.

    OKQ mfm (LP)   OPET mfm (L)
    OOU mfm (LP)

    Guide: Canada. Royal Commission on Canada's Economic Prospects <u>Index to Briefs and Transcripts of Public Hearings</u>. Toronto, Micromedia Ltd., 1972.

81. Canada. Royal Commission on Dominion-Provincial Relations. <u>Briefs and Transcripts, 1937-1938</u>. Ottawa, Public Archives, Central Microfilm Unit (for Micromedia) 1974.

    OKQ mfm (LP)   OPET mfm (L)
    OOU mfm (LP)   OTYL mfm

    Guide: Canada. Royal Commission on Dominion-Provincial Relations. <u>Index to Briefs and Transcripts of Public Hearings</u>. Toronto, Micromedia Ltd., 1973.

82. Canada. Royal Commission on Energy. <u>Briefs and Transcripts</u>. Ottawa, Public Archives of Canada Central Microfilm Unit (for Micromedia), 1973. 16 reels.

    OKQ mfm (LP)   OPET mfm (L)
    OOU mfm (LP)   OTY mfm

    Guide: Briefs (reel 1-10). Listed on each reel by volume. Master index also on each reel. <u>Transcripts</u> (reel 11-16). Index of transcripts on reel 11 in chronological order.

83. Canada. Royal Commission on National Development in the Arts, Letters and Sciences 1949-1951. <u>Briefs and Transcripts</u>. Toronto, Micromedia Ltd., 1972. 24 reels.

    OKQ mfm (LP)   OPET mfm (L)
    OOU mfm (LP)

    Guide: Canada. Royal Commission on National Development in the Arts, Letters and Sciences. <u>Index to Briefs and Transcripts of Public Hearings</u>. Toronto, Micromedia, Ltd., 1972.

84. Canada. Royal Commission on Taxation. <u>Briefs and Transcripts</u>. Ottawa, Public Archives Central Microfilm Unit (for Micromedia), 1974. 13 reels.

    Guide: Canada. Royal Commission on Taxation. <u>Index to Briefs and Transcripts of Public Hearings</u>. Toronto, Micromedia Ltd., 1974.

85. Canada. Royal Commission on the Status of Women. <u>Briefs and Transcripts</u>. Toronto, Micromedia, 1972. 6 reels.

    OOCC mfm (P)   OSTCB mfm (LP)
    OOU mfm (LP)   OTY mfm
    OPET mfm (L)

    Guide: Canada. Royal Commission on the Status of Women. <u>Index to Briefs and Transcripts of Public Hearings</u>. Toronto, Micromedia Ltd., 1972.

86. Canada. Royal Commission on the Status of Women. <u>Studies</u>. Ottawa, Public Archives of Canada, 1973. 6 reels.

    OKQ mfm (LP)   OSTCB mfm (LP)

    Guide: Public Archives Record Group 33/89 v.25-30. (Alphabetically by author).

87. Canada (Province) Department of Public Instruction for Upper Canada. Journal of Education for Upper Canada, 1848-1867. Ottawa.

    OSUL mfm (LP)

88. Canada (Province) Parliament. Legislative Assembly. Journal of the Legislative Assembly 1842-1866; Appendix to the Journals, 1842-1859; Sessional Papers, 1860-1866. Washington, D.C., United States 'Historical Documents Institute', 1972.

    OOCC mfm (Journals 1841-1866) (P)   OSUL mfm (LP)
    OOU   mfm (LP)
    OPET mfm (L)

    Guide: Canada Parliament. Legislative Assembly. General Index to the Journals of the Legislative Assembly of Canada, 1852-66. Ottawa, 1867. Includes Index to the Sessional Papers, 1860-1866.

89. Canada (Province) Parliament. Legislative Council. Journals, v.1-26, 1841-1866. Washington, D.C., United States 'Historical Documents Institute'. 1972.

    OOCC mfm   OTY mfm
    OPET mfm (L)   OWA mfm (LP)
    OSUL mfm (LP)   QMM mfm (1843-57)

    Guide: Canada (Province) Parliament. Legislative Council. Index to the Journals of the Legislative Council. 13 vols.

90. Canadian Federal Royal Commission Reports, 1867-1966. Toronto, Micromedia Ltd.

    OGU mfe   OOU mfe (LP)
    OLU mfe (LP)   QMM mfe (P)

    Guide: Henderson, George Fletcher. Federal Royal Commission in Canada 1867-1966: A Checklist. Toronto, University of Toronto Press, 1967.

91. Canadian Historical Documents. Part one. Quebec Literary and Historical Society Documents (1838-1915); Part Three. Documents from the Canadian Public Archives (1882-1902) Philadelphia, Penn., Academic Microforms, 1976.

    OWL mfe (L)

92. Canadian Imprints, 1751-1800, Identified and Arranged by Tremaine Numbers; Reproductions of Items Listed in Marie Tremaine's: A Bibliography of Canadian Imprints, 1751-1800. Ottawa, Public Archives of Canada Central Microfilm Unit, 1962. 21 reels.

    OLU mfm (LP)   OWTU mfm (LP)
    OOU mfm (LP)   QMG   mfm (L)
    OTU mfm (LP)   QMM   mfm (P)

    Guide: Tremaine, Marie. A Bibliography of Canadian Imprints, 1751-1800. Toronto, University of Toronto Press, 1952.

93. Canadian Library Assoc. Newspaper Microfilming Project. Canadian Newspapers on Microfilm. Ottawa, 1946-

    OGU   mfm (selected titles)
    OHM   mfm (LP)
    OKQ   mfm (selected titles) (LP)
    OLU   mfm (LP)
    OOCC   mfm (selected titles) (LP)
    OOU   mfm (LP)
    OPET   mfm (selected titles) (LP)
    OSTCB mfm (selected titles) (LP)
    OTU   mfm (LP)
    OWA   mfm (LP)
    OWL   mfm (selected titles) (L)
    QLB   mfm (selected titles)
    QMM   mfm (selected titles)
    QQLA   mfm (selected titles) (LP)

    Guide: Canadian Library Association. Microfilm Committee. Canadian Newspapers on Microfilm, a Catalogue. Ottawa, C.L.A., 1959- 3v. (loose leaf)

94. Canadian Music Centre, Toronto. Collection of Unpublished Canadian Musical Scores. Toronto, Canadian Music Centre, 1970. Microfilm. 31 reels.

    OHM mfm (LP)   QMM mfm (P)
    OWA mfm (P)

    Guide: Canadian Music Centre, Toronto. Catalogue of Microfilms of Unpublished Canadian Music. Toronto, 1970.

95. Canadian Northwest. New Haven, Conn., Research Publications, 1976. 20 reels.

    OWL mfm (L)

96. Canadian Publications in the Field of Urban and Regional Planning and Development. Toronto, Micromedia Ltd., 1977-

    OWTU mfe (LP)

97. Canadian Theses on Microfiche/Microfilm. Ottawa, National Library of Canada. (In Progress)

    OGU   mfe   (selected titles)
    OLU   mfm, mfe (selected titles) (LP)
    OSTCB mfm   (selected titles)
    OSUL   mfm   (LP)
    OWA   mfm   (LP)

    Guides: Canadian Theses on Microfilm Catalogue. Ottawa, National Library of Canada (and Supplements)
    Canadiana, Section 1, Part III, 1972; Section 1, Part II 1973-   Ottawa, National Library.

98. Canadian Urban Sources, 1973-75. Toronto, Micromedia Ltd.

    OGU mfe   OOCC mfe (P)
    OHM mfe (LP)   OTU   mfe (LP)
    OLU mfe

    Guides: Canadian Urban Sources Table of Contents Listing by Microfiche Accession Number. Toronto, Micromedia Ltd. and Canadian Council on Urban and Regional Research

    Urban and Regional References, 1973-1975/6. Ottawa, Urban Research Council of Canada.

99. Canadiana in the Toronto Public Library. Toronto, Public Library; Washington, Microcard Editions, 1966-

    OGU   mfe   OSTCB   mfe (P)
    OHM   mfe (LP)   OTU   mfe (has 1st group only) (LP)
    OOU   mfe (LP)   OWA   mfe (#1394 sheets) (LP)
    OPAL mfe (LP)   OWTU   mfe (has 1st group only) (LP)
                        QQLA   mfe (LP)
                        OSHERU mfe (L)

    Guide: Toronto. Public Library. A Bibliography of Canadiana (1534-1867) in the Toronto Public Library; Edited by Frances M. Staton and Marie Tremaine. Toronto, 1934; and First Supplement, Ibid., 1959.

100. Carleton, Sir Guy. <u>Historical Military Records of the British Army in the American Revolution, 1747-1783</u>. Microfilm of Photostats in Colonial Williamsburg Made by Micro Photo Division, Bell & Howell, Cleveland, 1957. 107v. in 30 reels.
Originals in Public Record Office, London.

    OTU mfm (LP)   QQLA mfm (LP)
    QMG mfm (L)

101. Carlyle, Thomas. <u>Correspondence of Thomas Carlyle and Mrs. Jane Carlyle from Carlyle's House, 24 Cheyne Row, Chelsea</u>. East Ardsley, Eng., Micro Methods Ltd., 1971.

    OTR mfm (L)

102. Carnegie-Myrdal Study: the <u>Negro in America</u>: Research Memoranda for use in the Preparation of Dr. Gunnar Myrdal's an American Dilemma, 1940. 50v. New York: New York Public Library; Millwood, N.Y.: Distributed by Kraus-Thomson, 1945. 13 reels and Index.

    OGU mfm

    Guide: The Preface to Myrdal's <u>an American Dilemma</u>. Lists These Thirty Research Memoranda, Deposited in the Schomburg Collection of the New York Public Library.

103. Catholic Church. <u>Congregation de Propaganda Fide, Acta, 1622-1862</u>.

    OTU mfm

104. Catholic Church in France. Assemblée Générale du Clergé. <u>Collection des Procès-Verbaux des Assemblées-Générales du Clergé de France Depuis L'Année 1560 Jusqu'à Présent</u>. Rédigés par Ordre de Matières et Réduits à ce Qu'ils Ont D'essentiel. Ouvrage Composé Sous la Direction de L'Evêque de Macon. Autorisé par les Assemblées de 1762 & 1763, & Imprimé par Ordre du Clergé. Paris, G. Desprez, 1767-80. Chicago, University of Chicago Library, Dept. of Photoduplication, 1971. 10 reels.

    OTU mfm (LP)

105. Challen, William Harold, comp. <u>Parish Register Typescripts</u>. Prepared by W.H. Challen from Parishes in London, Midlands & Southern Counties. London, Guildhall Library, 1969. 21 reels.

    OTU mfm

106. Charente-Maritime, France (Dept.) Archives Departementales. <u>Documents Appartenant aux Archives Departementales de la Gironde,</u> France. La Rochelle, Archives Departementales de la Charente-Maritime, France, 1967. 4 reels.

    OWA   mfm   (LP)

107. <u>Chatham Newspapers</u>, 1848-1942. Chatham, Ont. Public Library, 30 reels. N.B. Other Chatham Newspapers Included in Canadian Library Association's Newspaper Microfilming Project, 4 vols.

    OTU   mfm   (LP)   OWTU   mfm
    OWA   mfm   (11 reels)   (LP)

108. Chaucer, Geoffrey. <u>Chaucer Manuscripts</u>; Manly Collection in University of Chicago Libraries. Chicago, University of Chicago Libraries, Dept. of Photographic Reproduction (n.d.)

    OTU   mfm   (LP)

109. Chaucer Society, London. <u>Publications, Ser.1 and 2.</u> Washington, D.C. Microcard Editions, 523 cards.

    OHM   mcd   (LP)   OOU   mcd
    OKQ   mcd   (series II)   (L)

110. Ch'en, Ch'eng. <u>Shih-Sou Tzu Liao Shih Kung Fei Tzu Liao.</u> Standard, Calif., Stanford University, Hoover Institutions on War, Revolution and Peace, 1960.

    OTU   mfm   (LP)

111. Chicago, <u>University of (Theses, PhD)</u> Chicago, University of Chicago Library, Dept. of Photographic Reproduction 1934?-1947. 69 reels.

    OTU   mfm   (LP)

112. China. Inspectorate General of Customs. <u>Decennial Reports on the Trade, Navigation, Industries, etc. of the Ports Open to Foreign Commerce in China and Corea, and on the Condition and Development of the Treaty Port Provinces.</u> Shanghai, 1893-

    QMM   mfm   (1st-5th Report (1882-1931)   (P)

113. <u>Chinese Communism 1927-1964</u>: a Collection of Pamphlets Issued by
 Chinese Communist Leaders and Party Officials. Stanford, Calif.,
 Hoover Institution on War, Revolution and Peace. 65 reels.

   OKQ   mfm   (L)

114. <u>Chinese Culture Series</u>. Lexington, Ky., Erasmus Press, 1967-   Rare
 Editions of Chinese Classical Literature.

   OTU   mfm   (LP)   OWA   mfm   (LP)

115. Church Missionary Society. <u>Proceedings of the Church Missionary
 Society for Africa and the East</u>. London, 1801-1921. East Ardsley,
 Wakefield, Yorks., Micro Methods, 1967. 40 reels.

   OHM   mfm   (LP)

116. Church Missionary Society. <u>Records Relating to Africa, Circa 1803-
 1904/21</u>. East Ardsley, Yorks., Micro Methods, 1967. 40 reels.

   OHM   mfm   (LP)

117. Church Missionary Society. <u>West Indies Mission Records, 1819-1861</u>.
 East Ardsley, Yorks, Micro Methods. 1967. 14 reels.

   OHM   mfm   (LP)   OWTU   mfm   (LP)

118. Church Missionary Society. <u>Yoruba Mission; Niger Mission; South
 African Mission; East African Mission; Nyanza Mission; Kenya
 Mission. Committee Records</u>. Chicago, University of Chicago
 Library. Microfilm. Reels 52-276.

   QMM   mfm   (P)

119. Church of Geneva. <u>Ecclesiastical Correspondence</u>. N.Y., Recordax
 46 reels.

   QMM   mfm   (P)

120. Clare, John. <u>Manuscripts from the Collection in Northampton Central
 Library</u>. Wakefield, Eng., E.P. Microform Ltd., 1974. 11 reels.

   OGU   mfm   OKQ   mfm   (LP)

121. Claude Kitchin Papers in the Southern Historical Collection of the University of North Carolina Library. Chapel Hill, 1966.

   OOU mfm (LP)

122. Colbert, Jean-Baptiste. Lettres, Instruction Set Memoires de Colbert. Leportulan, Paris.

   OOU mfe (LP)

123. Collection Adrien Arcand. Montreal. Centre de Recherche en Histoire Economique du Canada Francais 1970? 6 reels.

   OTU mfm (LP)   QMG mfm (L)

124. Collection of Targum Manuscrips and Fragments. Toronto: Kodak Canada, 1976. 5 reels.

   OTU mfm

125. Communist Pary of Great Britain. Publications, Ser.1, Journals, 1921-1977, Ser.2, Newspapers, 1916-29., Ser.3, Theoretical Journals, 1921-1977, Ser.4, Pamphlets, 1920-77., With Printed Index. N.J. London, Eng., World Microfilm Publications.

   OHM mfe (LP)

126. La Condition Ouvrière en France au 19e Siècle. Paris, Micro Editions Hachette, 197-

   OKQ mfe (LP)

127. Congressional Information Service. CIS Microfiche Library. 1976- Washington, D.C.

   OKQ mfe

   Guide: CIS/Index to Publications of the United States Congress. Washington, D.C., Congressional Information Service Monthly- CIS/Annual. Vols. for 1970- Issued in 2 pts., 1. Abstracts of Congressional Publications and Legislative Histories. - 2. Index to Congressional Publications and Public Laws.

128. Conti, Antonio Schinella. <u>Selected Works; a Selection of 11 MSS. from the Biblioteca Comunale Vincenzo Joppi di Udine</u>. 11 reels.

    UTO   mfm   (LP)

129. Cook, James. <u>Log and Journal of Captain Cook's Voyage Round the World in the Bark 'Endeavour' 1768-1771</u>. East Ardsley, Yorks, Micro Methods Ltd. 1 reel.

    OTR   mfm   (L)

130. Cornell University. <u>Petrarch Collection</u>. Millwood, New York, Kraus-Thomson Organization, Ltd., 1973?

    OLU   mfe   (LP)

    Guide: Jennings, Laura. <u>Catalogue of the Petrarch Collection in Cornell University Library</u>. Millwood, New York, Kraus-Thomson Organization, Ltd., 1974.

131. Cornell University. Olin Library. <u>The Cornell University Collection of Women's Rights Pamphlets, 1814-1912</u>. Wooster, Ohio: Bell & Howell, 1973? 117 Microfiche and Index.

    OGU   mfe   OKQ   mfe   (LP)

132. <u>Corpus Scriptorum Ecclesiaticorum Latinorum</u>, vols. 1-60, 1866-1913. Washington, Microcard Editions, 1966.

    OWL   mfe   (L)

133. <u>Correspondance de Henri Bourassa Avec Laurier Sir Wildrid, Lavergne Armand, Milner Lord, Monk F.D., Tardivel J.P.</u> Ottawa, Service Central du Microfilm. Archives Publiques du Canada, 1967. 2 reels.

    QSHERU   mfm   (L)

134. <u>Covent Garden Prompt Books</u>. (v.p.) 37 v. Cleveland: Micro Photo Division, Bell & Howell, 1969. 3 reels.

    OHM   mfm   (LP)

135. Crime and Juvenile Delinquency. Glen Rock, N.J., Microfilming Corporation of America.

    OGU mfe

    Guide: Crime and Juvenile Delinquency: a Preliminary Checklist of the Titles in the Basic Collection. Glen Rock, N.J., Microfilming Corporation of America, 1975-   annual.

136. Cuba. Laws, Statutes, etc. Gaceta Official de la Republica de Cuba, April 1902-Oct. 1967. New York, Datamics, inc.

    OWTU mfe

137. Current National Statistical Compendiums, 1970-73. Westport, Conn., Greenwood Press, 1975.

    OGU mfe   OLU mfe (LP)

138. Daly's Fifth Avenue Theatre, New York. Bill of the Play; 1879-1892, 1896-97. New York, New York Public Library, 1961. 7 reels.

    OTU mfm (LP)

139. Daly's Fifth Avenue Theatre, Collection of Programs, 1879-1899. New York, New York Public Library, 1960. 1 reel.
    'Collection of Programmes, Newspaper Clippings, Playbills, etc.'

    OTU mfm (LP)

140. Daly's Fifth Avenue Theatre. New York. Correspondence and Documents, 1858-1899. New York, New York Public Library, 1961. Liechtenstein, Kraus Reprint, 1973. 3 reels.

    OTU mfm (LP)

141. Daly's Fifth Avenue Theatre. New York. Scrapbooks, 1863-1899. St. Paul, Minn., International Microfilm Press, 1967? 8 reels.

    OTU mfm (LP)

142. Dante Alighieri. Divina Comedia. East Ardsley, York, Micro Methods Ltd. 1 reel.

    OTR mfm (L)

143. Davis, Angela Yvonne. <u>Angela Davis Case Collection</u>. Bobbs Ferry, N.Y. Trans-Media Pub. Co., 1974. 13 reels.

   OGU mfm

144. The Declassified Documents Reference System. <u>Annual Collection</u>. Washington, D.C., Carrollton Press, Inc.

   OHM mfe (LP)   OLU mfe (LP)

   Guide: <u>The Declassified Documents Quarterly Catalogue</u>. (Abstracts and Cumulative Subject Index) Washington, D.C., Carrollton Press, Inc.

145. The Declassified Documents Reference System. <u>Retrospective Collection</u>. Washington, D.C., Carrollton Press, Inc.

   OHM mfe (LP)   OLU mfe (LP)

   Guide: The Declassified Documents Reference System. <u>Retrospective Collection</u>. Catalogue of Abstracts 2 vols. Washington, D.C., Carrollton Press, Inc., 1976.

146. Defoe, Daniel. <u>The Writings of Daniel Defoe</u>. London, University Microfilms Ltd., 1969. 38 reels.

   OLU mfm (LP)   OWL mfm (L)
   OTU mfm (LP)   QMG mfm (L)

   Guide: Moore, John Robert. <u>A Checklist of the Writings of Daniel Defoe</u>. Bloomington, Indiana, Indiana University Press, 1960.

147. De Groot, A.I., ed. <u>Library of Church Unity Periodicals</u>. Ser.1-3. Dallas, Microfilm Services & Sales 1964. 64 reels.

   OHM mfm (LP)   OWA mfm (1-3) (LP)

148. <u>Development Plans</u> (Social and Economic Development Plans D101-859) Zug, Switzerland; Inter Documentation Co., 1970. '750 texts of plans from 161 countries'.

   OOCC mfe (P)
   OTU   mfm
   QMM   mfe (119 titles from 57 countries) (P)

149. D'Holbach et ses Amis, 1760-1789. Paris, Micro Editions Hachette, c1972-73.

    OKQ   mfe   (LP)   OSTCB   mfe   (LP)

150. Dibdin, Thomas John. The London Theatre; a Collection of the Most Celebrated Dramatic Pieces. London, Printed for Whittingham and Arliss, 1815 (1814-25) 12 vols. 103 fiche.

    OKQ   mfe   (LP)

151. Dickens, Charles. Annotated Proofs of the Works of Charles Dickens from the Forster Collection in the Victoria and Albert Museum. East Ardsley Eng., Micro Methods Ltd. 1969. 3 reels.

    OHM   mfm   (LP)   OTR   mfm   (L)
    OSUL mfm   (LP)

152. Dickens, Charles. Manuscripts of the Works of Charles Dickens from the Forster Collection in the Victoria and Albert Museum, London. East Ardsley, Eng., Micro Methods, 1969. 7 reels.

    OHM   mfm   (3 reels)   (LP)   OSUL   mfm   (P)
    OKQ   mfm   (LP)

153. Dickens, Charles. Original Letters of Charles Dickens in the Dickens House. East Ardsley, Eng., Micro Methods, 197-   1 reel.

    OHM   mfm   (LP)

154. Dickens, Charles. Original Manuscripts of Charles Dickens and Other Papers: from Dickens House, London Introduction by Leslie C. Staples. -- East Ardsley, Eng.: Micro Methods, 197-

    OHM   mfm   (LP)   OTR   mfm   (L)

155. Diplomatic Correspondence of British Ministers to the Russian Court at St. Petersburg 1704-1776. Herts, England, Chadwyck-Healey Ltd.

    OLU   mfe   (LP)

    Guide: Chronological Index to the Diplomatic Correspondence of British Ministers to the Russian Court at St. Petersburg 1704-1776. Herts, Eng., Chadwyck-Healey Ltd., 1973.

156. <u>Documentry History of the Ratification of the Constitution.</u> Edited by Merrill Jensen. Madison: State Historical Society of Wisconsin, 1976-

   OWA   mfm   (v.1, v.2 and Supplement (LP)

157. <u>Documents de la Session du Quebec, 1924-1972.</u> Quebec. Service de Microfilm du Quebec.

   QSHERU   mfm   (L)

158. <u>Dod's Parliamentary Companion 1833-1909.</u> Washington, D.C., Microcard Editions, 1965-

   OTU   mfm/mfe   (P)

159. <u>Dod's Parliamentary Companion, 1911-1952.</u> Ann Arbor, University Microfilms, 1969?

   OTU   mfm   (P)

160. Dodsley, Robert, comp. <u>A Select Collection of Old English Plays.</u> Washington, D.C., Microcard Editions, n.d. 143 fiche.

   OKQ   mfe   (LP)

161. Dumont, Jean. <u>Corps Universel Diplomatique du Droit des Gens, 1726-1731.</u> Washington, D.C., Microcard Editions. 281 Fiche. Supplement, 1739. 5 vols. Washington, D.C., Microcard Editions. 157 Fiche.

   QLB   mfe   (L)

162. <u>Early American Imprints, First Series, 1639-1800</u>; Clifford K. Shipton, Evans no.1-   New York, Readex Microprint Corp. 1955-

   OLU   mpt   (L)   OWTU   mpt   (L)
   OTU   mpt   (LP)   QMM   mpt

   Guide: Bristol, Roger P. <u>Supplement to Chas. Evans' American Bibliography.</u> Charlottesville, Published for the Bibliographical Society of America and the Bibliographical Society of University of Virginia by University Press of Virginia, 1970.

   Evans, Charles. <u>American Bibliography... 1639 down to and Including the Year 1820.</u> Chicago 1903-1959. 14v.

162.   (Cont'd)

       Guide: New York Public Library. Rare Book Division. <u>Checklist of Additions to Evans' American Bibliography in the Rare Book Division</u>. Compiled by Lewis M. Stark and Maud D. Cole, New York Public Library, 1960.

       Shipton, Clifford Kenyon. <u>National Index of American Imprints Through 1800; the Short-Title Evans by Clifford K. Shipton and James E. Mooney</u>. Worcester, Mass., American Antiquarian Society, 1969. 2v.

163.   <u>Early American Imprints</u>, Second Series (Shaw-Shoemaker) 1801-1819. New York, Readex Microprint Corp., 1964-

      OLU   mpt   (L)   OTU   mpt   (LP)

       Guide: Bristol, Roger P. <u>Supplement to Charles Evans' American Bibliography</u>. Charlottesville, Published for the Bibliographical Society of America and the Bibliographical Society of University of Virginia, (by) University Press of Virginia 1970.

       Shaw, Ralph R. <u>American Bibliography: A Preliminary Checklist for 1801-1819</u>. Compiled by Ralph R. Shaw and Richard H. Shoemaker, New York, Scarecrow Press. 1858-1966.

164.   <u>Early American-Medical Imprints, 1668-1820</u>. New Haven, Conn., Research Publications Inc., 1973.

      OLU   mfm

       Guide: Austin, Robert B. <u>Early American Medical Imprints, 1668-1820</u>. Washington, D.C., 1951. New Haven, Conn., Research Publications, 1973.

       <u>Reel Index to the Microfilm Collection of Early American Medical Imprints, 1668-1820</u>. New Haven, Conn., Research Publications, 1973

165.   <u>Early English Text Society Publications, Original Series</u>. Nos.1-47. Washington, D.C., Microcard Editions.

      OHM   mcd   (L)

166.   <u>Early Toronto Planning Documents</u>. Toronto, Metropolitan Toronto Library Board, s.d. 10 Fiche.

      OKQ   mfe   (LP)

167. East India Company. A Calendar of the Court Minutes etc. of the East India Company, 1635-79, by Ethel Bruce Sainsbury. Tumba, International Documentation Centre, 1969? 89 fiche.

   OWA   mfe   (LP)

168. Economics Working Papers. Dobbs Ferry, N.Y.: Trans-Media Pub. in Association with University of Warwick.

   OOCC   mfe   (Earlier mfe now mfm)   (LP)
   OWTU   mfe   (Earlier mfe now mfm)   (LP)

   Guide: Author, Subject and Series Index in Economics Working Papers Bibliography.

169. Educational Testing Service. Tests in Microfiche. Princeton, N.J., Educational Testing Service, 1975-

   OGU   mfe   (set A, pt.1-2, set B, pt.1-2)

170. Eichmann, Adolf. Transcript of the Trial in the Case of the Attorney-General of the Government of Israel VS Adolf, the Son of Adolf Karl Eichmann, in the District Court of Jerusalem. Criminal Case no. 40/61. Washington, D.C., Microcard Editions 1962. 139 fiche.

   OHM   mfe   (LP)

171. Eighteenth Century Russian Publications on Microfilm, 1725-1800. Lexington, Ky., Erasmus Press, Slavic Reprint Division, 1965-

   OTU   mfm   (LP)

   Guide: Svodnyi Katalog Russkoi Knigi Grazhdanskoi Pechati XVIII Veka, 1725-1800. Redaktsionnaia Kollegira: I.P. Kondakov i dr. Sostaviteli E.I. Katspizhak i dr. Moskva, 1962-67.

172. Eighteenth Century Sources for the Study of English Literature. Scotsville, Va., 2-M Microfilm Service, 1968.

   OLU   mfm   (LP)   OWA   mfm   (LP)
   OTU   mfm   (LP)

173. English and American Drama of the 19th Century; American Plays, 1831-1900. English Plays, 1801-1900. Edited by George Freedley and Allardyce Nicoll. New York, Readex Microprint Corp. 1965?

173.   (Cont'd)

    OGU mpt   OTU mpt (LP)
    OHM mpt (L)   OWA mpt

Guides: Nicoll, Allardyce. <u>A History of English Drama 1660-1900</u>. 6 vols. 4th Ed. London: Cambridge University Press, 1952-59.

Quinn, Arthur Hobson. <u>A History of the American Drama from the Beginning to the Civil War</u>. 2d. ed. New York: Appleton-Century-Crofts, 1943.

Quinn, Arthur Hobson. <u>A History of the American Drama from the Civil War to the Present Day</u>. Rev. ed. New York: Irvington, 1946.

Roden, Robert F. <u>Later American Plays 1831-1900: Being a Compilation of the Titles of Plays by American Authors Published and Performed in America Since 1831-1900</u>. Reprint. New York: B. Franklin, 1964.

Von Chorba, Albert. <u>Checklist of American Drama Published in the English Colonies of North America and the United States Through 1865</u>, in the Possession of the Library, University of Pennsylvania, 1951.

174. <u>English Books, 1475-1640</u>. Ann Arbor, Mich., University Microfilms, 1938.

    OGU   mfm   OTU   mfm   (LP)
    OHM   mfm (LP)   OWA   mfm   (LP)
    OKQ   mfm (LP)   OWTU mfm   (LP)
    OLU   mfm (LP)   QMG   mfm   (L)
    OOU   mfm (LP)   QMM   mfm   (P)
    OPAL mfm (LP)

Guides: Pollard, A.W. <u>A Short-Title Catalogue of Books Printed in England, Scotland and Ireland and of English Books Printed Abroad 1475-1640</u>, Compiled by A.W. Pollard and G.R. Redgrave. London, Bibliographical Society, 1926.

University Microfilms, Ann Arbor, Mich. <u>English Books, 1475-1640</u>. A Partial List by STC Numbers. 1938- Annual with 5 - year Cumulations.

175. English Books 1641-1700. Ann Arbor, Mich. University Microfilms

    OGU mfm   OPAL mfm reels 267-301 (LP)
    OHM mfm (LP)   OTU   mfm (LP)
    OKQ mfm (LP)   OWA   mfm reels 79, 95-161, 302-338-
    OLU mfm (LP)   (LP)
    OOU mfm (LP)   OWTU mfm (LP)
                                    QMG   mfm (L)

    Guides:University Microfilms, Ann Arbor, Mich. English Books,
        1641-1700; a Partial List by Wing Numbers. 1961-
        Annual with five Years Cummulation.

    Wing, Donald G. Short Title Catalogue of Books Printed in
    England... 1641-1700. New York, Printed for Index Society
    by Columbia University Press, 1945.

    Wing, Donald G. Short Title Catalogue of Books Printed in
    England ... 1641-1700. New York, Modern Language Associa-
    tion, 1972.

176. English Experience, Group 1-10. Norwood, N.J., W.J. Johnson.

    OWL mfe (L)

    Guide: Pollard, A.W. A Short-Title Catalogue of Books Printed in
        England, Scotland, and Ireland and of English Books Printed
    Abroad 1475-1640, Compiled by A.W. Pollard and G.R. Redgrave.
    London, Bibliographical Society, 1926.

177. English Literary Periodicals, 1600-1900. Ann Arbor, Mich., University Microfilms.

    OKQ mfm (L)   OWTU mfm (LP)
    OLU mfm (LP)   QMG   mfm (L)
    OTU mfm (each title catalogued separately)

    Guide: Bond, Richmond Pubh. Studies in the Early English Periodical.
    Chapel Hill, University of North Carolina Press, 1957.

    English Literary Periodicals 17th, 18th, and 19th Centuries.
    (A Guide to the Contents) Ann Arbor, Mich., University
    Microfilms, 1951-   1v. (loose leaf)

178. English Reports. Full Reprint. Washington, D.C., Microcard Editions, 1966-68. 176v. and 2v. Index.
    All law reports for 1378-1865 as contained in some 274 different series, e.g. House of Lords, Chancery Court, Rolls Court, Kings Bench, etc.

    OGU mfe   OHM mfe (LP)

179. Envirofiche, v.1, 1971-____. New York, Microfiche Systems Corp.

    OWTU   Mfe   (L)

    Guides: Environment Abstracts. New York: Environment Information Center, 1974.

    Environment Index. New York: Environment Information Center

180. European Official Statistical Serials on Microfiche, Herts, Eng., Chadwyck-Healey Ltd., 1975-   .

    OHM   mfe   (LP)   OKQ   mfe   (Annuaire Statistique de la Belgique. (L)
                            OTU   mfm

181. Evangelical Academies and Lay Training Centers of Europe and Great Britain. Historical Sketches, Conference Programs, Announcement Bulletins, Studyguides and Other Representative Publications of These Centers. Edited by A.T. De Groot, Fort Worth, Texas, Texas Christian University, 1967. 1967. 11 reels.

    OWL   mfm   (L)

182. Evans, (Sir) Arthur John. Evans and Mackenzie Note Books, 1900-1929. East Ardsley, Wakefield, Yorks., Micro Methods 1965? 3 reels.

    OTU   mfm   (LP)

183. FLQ. Clipping from Canadian Newspapers and Magazines, 1970-71, by the Canadian Press Clipping Service. Toronto: Maclean Hunter Microfilm Services. 1 reel.

    OHM   mfm   (LP)

184. Fabian Society, London. Minute Books, 1884-1918. Hassocks, Eng.; Harvester Press, 1975. 141 fiche.

    OPAL   mfe   (LP)

185. Fabian Society Tracts, 1884-1942. Yorkshire, England, EP Microform Ltd. 1974.

    OHM   mfm   1884-   35 reels.   (LP)
    OLU   mfm   (nos.1-427)   (LP)
    OTR   mfm   (nos. 306, 711, 2434, 4685, 96301) 6 reels.   (L)

186. Faillon, Etienne Michel. <u>Fonds Faillon.</u> Index 1677-1834. Montreal, Seminaire Saint-Sulpice. s.d. Montreal, Societe Canadienne de Microfilm, 1968. 8 reels.

    QHERU mfm (L)

187. <u>Files of Evidence Connected with the Investigation of the Assassination of President John F. Kennedy.</u> n.p. 1963-64. Washington, D.C., Microcard Editions. 2 reels.

    OTU mfm (LP)

188. <u>Finney Papers, 1792-1875.</u> Oberlin Ohio, Oberlin College, s.d. 9 reels.

    OKQ   (LP)

189. Finnish Organization of Canada. <u>Finnish-Canadian Play and Operetta Manuscript Collection.</u> Toronto, McLaren Micro Publishing, 1974. 76 fiche.

    OPAL mfe (LP)   OTU mfe (LP)

    Guide: Accompanied by Printed Finding Aid (8p.)

190. Florence. Biblioteca Nazionale Centrale. <u>La Collezione Palatina (de Commedia, Drammi, Pastorali, Tragedie e Drammi Spirituali, Tragicommedie e di Pescatorie e Marittime).</u> Centro di Microschedatura e di Documentazione Internationale Fotomicrografica, 1962- 104 vols. on 155 reels; 119v. on 175 reels.

    OTU mfm

    Guide: <u>Studi Secenteschi, v.2-7, 9 etc.</u> (Bibliographies Each on a Particular Part of the Collezione Palatina)

191. Foster, Sir William. <u>The English Factories in India; a Calendar of Documents in India Office, British Museum and Public Record Office.</u> Published Under the Patronage of His Majesty's Secretary of State for India in Council. Oxford, Clarendon Press, 1906-1955, Tumba, International Documentation Centre, 1969? 130 fiche. (Period covered 1618-1684)

    OWA mfe (LP)

192. <u>Four Centuries of Spanish Drama: 1500-1900</u>. v.p., 1600-19- Washington, D.C., Microcard Editions, Inc., 1959-

    OTU   mcd   (LP)

    Guide: Thompson, L.S. <u>A Bibliography of Spanish Plays on Microcards</u>. Hamden, Conn., Shoe String Press, 1968.

193. France. <u>Journal Officiel de la Republique Francaise 1869-1880</u>. Washington, N.C.R. Microcard Editions.

    OHM   mfm   (LP)   OTU   mcd   (P)
    OOCC mfe   (P)   OTY   mfm
    OOU   mfe   (LP)   OWTU mfm   (P)

194. France. <u>Journal Officiel de la République Française Sous la Commune 1871 Paris</u>. L'Association Pour la Conservation et la Reproduction Photographique de la Presse (A.C.R.P.P.) 1961. 1 reel.

    OSUL mfm

195. France. Assemblée Nationale 1871-1942. Chambre des Deputes. <u>Débats Parlementaires, 1881-1940</u>. Paris, Association Pour la Conservation et la Reproduction Photographique de la Presse, 1962-64.

    OHM   mfm   (LP)   OTU   mcd   (P)
    OOCC mfe   (P)   OTY   mfm
    OOU   mfm   (LP)   OWTU mfm 165 reels (P)

196. France. Assemblée Nationale 1871-1942. Chambre des Deputés. <u>Documents Parlementaires, Sessions Ordinaires: 1881-1938. Sessions Extraordinaires: 1885, 1888-1890, 1893, 1898-1910, 1911-1914, 1919-1938</u>. Paris, ACRPP.

    OWTU mfm   (148 reels)   (P)

197. France. Commission de Publication des Documents Relatifs aux Origines de la Guerre de 1914. <u>Documents Diplomatiques Français, (1871-14)</u> Paris, Impr. Nationale, 1929-59.

    OOCC mfe   (Publisher, Wooster, Ohio, Bell and Howell Co.) (P)
    OPAL mfe   (Series 1-3) 511 fiche (L)

198. France. Conseil de Depêches. <u>Repertoire Chronologique et Analytique des Arrêts du Conseil des Depêches 1611-1710</u>. Paris, S.I.M. Service International de Microfilms. 20 reels.

    OTU mfm   QMM mfm (P)

199. France. Ministre de L'Agriculture et du Commerce. <u>Annuaire Statistique, 1878-1965</u>. N.J., Somerset House.

    OSUL mfe (LP)

200. Franklin Institute, Philadelphia. Committee on Science and the Arts. <u>Records of the Committee on Science and the Arts of the Franklin Institute, 1824-1900</u>. Wilmington, Delaware, Scholarly Resources, 1977.

    OWL mfm (L)

    Guide: McMahon, A. Michael and Stephanie A. Morris. <u>Technology in Industrial America: the Committee on Science and the Arts of the Franklin Institute, 1824-1900</u>. Wilmington, Delaware, Scholarly Resources, 1977.

201. <u>French Books Before 1601</u>. Lexington, Ky., Erasmus Press, 1965-

    OGU mfm 140 reels   OOU mfm (Ann Arbor, University Microfilm (LP)

    Guide: British Museum. Dept. of Printed Books. <u>Short-Title Catalogue of Books Printed in France and of French Books Printed in Other Countries from 1470 to 1600 in the British Museum</u>. London, 1966.

202. <u>French Revolutionary Materials, Maclure Collection, Univ. of Pennsylvania</u>. New Haven, Conn., Research Publications.

    OLU mfm (LP
    OKQ mfm (v.1-1005, 1009-1012, 1017-1460) (LP)
    OOCC mfm (v.1-488) (LP)
    OTY mfm v.1-
    QQLA mfm (LP)

    Guide: Pennsylvania. University. Library. <u>The Maclure Collection of French Revolutionary Materials</u>, ed. by James D. Hardy, John H. Jensen, and Martin Wolfe. Philadelphia, Univ. of Philadelphia Press, 1966.

203. French Revolutionary Pamphlets on Microcards. Louisville, Falls City Microcard, 1961-

    OGU mcd/mfe   OTU mcd/mfe (LP)
    OHM mcd (L)   QMG mcd
    OKQ mfe (L)   QQLA mcd (L)

Guides: New York (City) Public Library. French Revolutionary Pamphlets; a Checklist of the Talleyrand and Other Collections, Compiled by Horace E. Hayden, Under the Direction of Charles F. McCombs. New York, New York Public Library, 1945.

Saricks, Ambrose. A Bibliography of the Frank E. Melvin Collection of Pamphlets of the French Revolution in the University of Kansas Libraries. 2 vols. Lawrence: University of Kansas Libraries, 1960.

Thompson, Lawrence S.A. Bibliography of French Revolutionary Pamphlets on Microfiche. Troy, N.Y.: Whitston, 1974.

204. Fritsch, Felix Eugene. Fritsch Collection of Algae. Zug, Switzerland: Inter-Documentation Co., AG., 1974. 1181 fiche.

    OGU mfe

205. Gallatin, Albert. The Papers of Albert Gallatin, Sponsored by New York University and National Historical Publications Commission. Wilmington, Del., Scholarly Resources, 1969. 46 reels.

    OWA mfm (LP)

206. Garden, Guillaume de. Histoire Générale des Traites de Paix et Autres Transactions Principales Entre Toutes les Puissances de L'Europe Depuis la Paix de Westphalie. Paris, Amyot, 1848-1887. 107 fiche.

    QLB mfe (L)

207. Garrick, David. Collected Correspondence and Miscellaneous Papers of David Garrick, 1717-1779. East Ardsley, Yorkshire, Micro Methods, 1969. 10 reels.
'from the Forester collection of the Victoria and Albert Museum, London.'

    OHM mfm (LP)   QMM mfm (P)
    OTR mfm (L)

208. Gay, Ebenezer, ed. Early American Newspapers, 1704-1820. Worcester, Mass., American Antiquarian Society, 1959?   v.1-   The Boston Chronicle, 1767-1770; The Massachusetts Spy, 1770-1775; Censor, 1771-72. 54 cards.

    OKQ   mcd   (L)

209. The German Army High Command, 1938-1945. Arlington, Va., University Publications of America, 1975. 4 reels.

    OWL   mfm   (L)

210. German Baroque Literature; Harold Jantz Collection. New Haven, Research Publications, 1973. 611 reels.

    OOCC   mfm   (LP)   OTU   mfm   (LP)

    Guide: German Baroque Literature; a Descriptive Catalogue and Guide to the Collection on Microfilm. Haven, Conn., Research Publications, 1974.

211. German Baroque Literature; Yale University Collection. New Haven, Research Publications, Inc., 1969-   656 reels.

    OGU   mfm   OTU   mfm   (LP)
    OLU   mfm   (LP)   OWTU   mfm   (LP)
    OOCC mfm   (LP)   QMM   mfm   (P)

    Guide: Faber du Faur, Curt von. German Baroque Literature: a Catalogue of the Collection in the Yale University Library. New Haven, Yale University Press, 1958-1969. 2v.

212. German Books Before 1601. Lexington, Ky., Erasmus Press, 1965

    OGU   mfm   (Reels 125)

    Guide: British Museum. Dept. of Printed Books. Short-Title Catalogue of Books Printed in the German-Speaking Countries... from 1455 to 1600 now in the British Museum. London, 1962.

213. The German Classics of the Nineteenth and Twentieth Centuries. Masterpieces of German Literature tr. into English. Editor in-Chief: Kuno Francke ... Assistant Editor-in-Chief: William Guild Howard. New York, c1913-14. Washington, D.C., Brookhaven Press.

    OHM   mfm   (LP)

214. German Confederation, 1815-1866. Bundesversammlung. <u>Protkolle der Detuschen Bundesversammlung, 1816-1866.</u> Frankfurt am Main 1817-67? 24v. Washington, Microcard Editions, 1964.

    OLU mcd (LP)   OTU mcd (LP)

    Guides: <u>Alphabetisches Hauptregister Uber die Protokolle der Deutschen Bundesversammlung, Erste Fortsetzung, die Verhandlungen vom Jahr 1937 Bis zum Schlusse des Jahrs 1846 Enthaltend.</u> Frankfurt a.m., Bundes-Prasidial - Budhdruckerei (1837?-46?) (included in the collection)

    <u>Alphabetisches Register Uber die Verhandlungen der Deutschen Bundesversammlung, vom. 1. October 1816 zum Schlusse des Jahrs 1836.</u> Frankfurt a.m. Bundes - Prasidial - Buchdruckerei 1817?-1837?) (included in the collection)

215. <u>German Drama on Microcards</u>, v.p., 1700-19. Washington D.C., Microcard Edition Inc., 1961-64. Louisville, Ky., Falls City Microcards, 1965-1970.

    OTU mcd/mfe (LP)

    Guide: Binger, Norman. <u>A Bibliography of German Plays on Microcards.</u> Hamden, Connecticut, The Shoestring Press, Inc., 1970.

216. Germany. Auswartiges Amt. <u>German Foreign Ministry Archives.</u> Washington, D.C., National Archives.

    OLU mfm (LP)   QMM mfm (P)

217. Germany. Auswartiges Amt. <u>German Foreign Ministry Archives, 1867-1920.</u> Berkeley, Calif., Univ. of California.

    OLU mfm (LP)

218. Germany. Auswartiges Amt. <u>German Foreign Ministry Archives, 1885-20.</u> Oxford, St. Antony's College.

    OLU mfm (LP)

    Guides: American Historical Association. Committee for the Study of War Documents. <u>A Catalogue of Files and Microfilms of the German Foreign Ministry Archives 1867-1920.</u> Washington 1959.

    U.S. Dept. of State. Historical Office. <u>A Catalog of the Files and Microfilms of the German Foreign Ministry Archives, 1920-1945.</u> Stanford, Calif., Stanford University, 1962.

219. Germany, Auswartiges Amt. Politisches Archiv. n.p., n.d. Washington, National Archives of the United States, n.d. 43 reels.

    QMM mfm (P)

220. Germany. Reichstag. Verhandlungen des Reichstags, 1867-79. Washington, D.C., Microcard Editions, 1963.

    OLU mcd (LP)   OTU mcd (LP)

221. Germany (Allied Occupation, 1945-1949). International Military Tribunal. Trial of the Major War Criminals Before the International Military Tribunal Nuernberg 14 Nov. 1945-1 Oct. 1946. N.Y. AMS Press.

    OWTU mfm (Blue series) (LP)

222. Germany (Allied Occupation, 1945-1949). International Military Tribunal. Trail of War Criminals Before the Nuernberg Military Tribunals Under Control Council Law no.10. N.Y., AMS Press.

    OWTU mfm (Green series) (LP)

223. The Gerristsen Collection of Women's History, 1543-1945. Glen Rock, N.J.: Microfilm Corporation of America, 1976-

    OHM mfe (LP)

224. Gloucester Cathedral. Mediaeval Registers of St. Peter's Abbey, Gloucester, with Abbot Frocester's History of the Abbey. Wakefield, England, Micro Methods, 196 ? 2reels.

    OKQ mfm (LP)

225. Goldsmith'-Kress Library of Economic Literature: Resources in the Economic, Social, Business and Political History of Modern Industrial Society. Segment 1: Printed Books Through 1800. New Haven, Conn., Research Publications, 1974. 789 reels.

    QMG mfm (some gaps) (L)

    Guides: Canney, Margaret, and Knott, David. Catalogue of the Goldsmiths' Library of Economic Literature: With an Introduction by J.H.P. Pafford. London, Cambridge University Press, 1970.

225.   (Cont'd)

Goldsmiths-Kress Library of Economic Literature: A Consolidated Guide to Segment 1 of the Microfilm Collection. Woodbridge, Conn.: Research Publications, 1976.

Harvard University. Graduate School of Business Administration. Baker Library. Kress Library of Business and Economics. The Kress Library of Business and Economics: Catalogue with Data Upon Cognate Items in Other Harvard Libraries. 4 vols. Boston: Harvard Graduate School of Business Administration, Baker Library, 1940-67.

226. Graf, Oskar Maria. Nachlass. Papers, 1933-67: Correspondence, MSS. of Novels, Peoms, Short Stories, Essays and Speeches, Many of Which are Unpublished, Photos, Clippings and Memorabilia Held in University of New Hampshire Library. University of New Hampshire Library, 1973. 12 reels.

QMM   mfm   (P)

227. Great Britain. Bulletins and Other State Intelligence, Compiled and Arranged from the Official Documents Published in the London Gazette. London. West Salem, Wis., Microcard Editions 1967. 10 reels.

OHM   mfm   (LP)

228. Great Britain. Royal Commission Reports Relating to Trades and Labour 1824-1894. Wakefield, Yorks, England, Micro Methods Ltd.

OSTCB   mfm   (LP)

229. Great Britain. Board of Customs and Excise. Ledgers of Exports of Foreign and Colonial Merchandise Under Countries, 1808-1899. (Customs 10) London, Public Record Office, 1974.

OLU   mfm   (custom 10 pce. nos. 62, 64, 66, 68)
QMM   mfm   (97v. on 5 reels)   (P)

230. Great Britain. Board of Customs and Excise. Ledgers of Imports and Exports, States of Navigation, Commerce and Revenue, 1772-1808. (Customs 17 pce. nos. 1-30) London, Public Record Office.

OLU   mfm   QMM   mfm   9 reels   (P)

231. Great Britain. Board of Customs and Excise. <u>Ledgers of Imports Under Countries, 1792-1899</u>. (customs 4) London, Public Record Office, 1975. Microfilm.

    QMM mfm (94 vols. 34 reels) (P)

232. Great Britain. Board of Trade. <u>Census of Production, 1907-1967</u>. London, Chadwyck-Healey Ltd.

    OLU mfm (LP)   OWTU mfm 113 reels (P)

233. Great Britain. Cabinet Office. <u>Cabinet Reports from Prime Ministers to the Crown 1868-1916</u>. Hassocks, London, Eng., Harvester Press, 1974. 14 reels.

    OHM   mfm (LP)   OSTCB mfm (LP)
    OKQ   mfm (LP)   OWTU   mfm
    OLU   mfm (LP)   QMM   mfm (P)

234. Great Britain. Cabinet Office. <u>Photographic Copies of Cabinet Papers, 1880-1916</u>. London, Public Record Office.

    OHM mfm (LP)

235. Great Britain. Central Statistical Office. <u>Annual Abstract of Statistics</u>. v.1-83., 1840-1938. Washington, Microcard Editions. 347 fiche.

    OPAL mfe (LP)

236. Great Britain. Colonial Office. <u>America and West Indies, Original Correspondence .... etc. 1606-1808</u>. London, Public Record Office, 1972.

    OWTU mfm (10 reels)

237. Great Britain. Colonial Office. <u>Annual Report on the Colonies, 1889-1939</u>. New York, Andronicus Publ. Co., 1975.

    OLU   mfe (LP)
    OWTU mfm
    QMM   mfm (Has Asian and Pacific Basin, Europe, Middle East and Miscelleneous) (P)

238. Great Britain. Colonial Office. Original Correspondence. (With Canada)
v.1-   1763-   London, Public Record Office, 105 reels.

   OKQ mfm (v.1-116, 1763-1800, v.477-572, 1841-1851)

   Guide: C.O. 42, v.1-22, 51 were Calendared in Canada Public Archives
   Report, 1921, Appendix D.

239. Great Britain. Exchequer. Memoranda Rolls of the Exchequer, 1218-1307.
London Public Record Office 1964? 17 reels.

   OTU mfm (LP)

240. Great Britain. Exchequer and Audit Dept. American Loyalist Claims,
Series 2, 1776-1831. London Public Record Office, 1972. 30 reels.

   OWTU mfm (P)

241. Great Britain. Exchequer and Audit Dept. American Loyalist Claims,
Series 2, 1776-1831. London, Public Record Office, 1973. 147 reels.

   OWTU mfm (reels 114-147 missing) (P)

242. Great Britain. Foreign and Commonwealth Office. Colonial Numbered
Series, 1924-60. Toronto, Micromedia.

   OWTU mfe

243. Great Britain Foreign and Commonwealth Office. Colonial Research
Publications. N.Y., K.T.O. Microform.

   OWTU mfe (nos. 1-13, 15, 17-25, 1948-1961)

244. Great Britain. Foreign Office. British and Foreign State Papers,
1812/14-1939. Washington, D.C., Microcard Editions, 1969.

   OGU mfe   OLU mfe (LP)
   OHM mfe (1812/14-1934) (LP)

245. Great Britain. Foreign Office. Confidential Prints on ... London,
Public Record Office, 1965; Washington, D.C., Microcard Editions.

   OHM   mcd Miscellaneous Colonial Conference, 1887, & North America,
              American Civil War. (L)
   OKQ   mfm South Africa up to 1916. Ser. co. 417, 879. (LP)
   OWTU mcd Miscellaneous Colonial Conference, 1887. (L)

246. Great Britain. Foreign Office. Confidential Prints on China, 1848-1937. London, Public Record Office, 1970.

   QMM mfm (P)

   Guide: Columbia University. East Asian Institute. A Guide to British Foreign Office: Confidential Print: China, 1848-1922. New York, 1970.

247. Great Britain. Foreign Office. Confidential Prints on China and the Far East, 1857-1915. London, Public Records Office, 1965.

   OTU mfm (LP)

   Guides: Great Britain. Foreign Office. Confidential Prints on China and the Far East, 1857-1915. London, Public Records Office, 1965.

   Great Britain. Foreign Office. Foreign Office Confidential Papers Relating to China and Her Neighbouring Countries, 1840-1914, with an Additional List 1915-1937. Compiled by Lo Hui-Min (Maison des Sciences de L'Homme) The Hague, Paris, Mouton, 1969.

248. Great Britain. Foreign Office. Correspondence with Her Majesty's Envoy Extraordinary Minister Plenipotentiary in Japan, August 1859-1910. London, Public Record Office. 6 reels.

   OTU mfm (LP)

249. Great Britain. Foreign Office. Foreign Office Records FO 800, Private Collections, Various Ministers and Officials, 1824-1949; Landsdowne Papers, 1898-1926. Nendeln, Kraus-Thomson, 1973.

   QMM mfm (FO 800/115-116, Landsdowne Papers; 1898-1926) (P)

250. Great Britain. Foreign Office Registers. (n.p., 1822-90) 13 v. London, Gt. Brit. Public Record Office, 1965. 5 reels.

   OTU mfm (LP)

251. Great Britain. Foreign Office. General Correspondence Before 1906. Archives of Conferences, 1813-1822. Toronto, Micromedia, 1977. 14 reels.

   OWL mfm (L)

252. Great Britain. Foreign Office. <u>General Correspondence Before 1906, China 1815-1850</u>. London, Public Record Office, 1972. 72 reels.

   OWTU mfm (P)

253. Great Britain. Foreign Office. <u>General Correspondence Before 1906, Continent Conferences, 1814-1822</u>. Toronto, Micromedia, 1977. 16 reels.

   OWL mfm (L)

254. Great Britain. Foreign Office. <u>General Correspondence Before 1906, Slave Trade 1816-1892</u>. N.Y., KTO Microforms. 1024 reels.

   OWTU mfm (P)

255. Great Britain. Foreign Office. <u>General Correspondence Before 1906, United States of America. Series 1, 1782-1795</u>. London, Public Record Office 1972. 10 reels.

   OWTU mfm (P)

256. Great Britain. Historical Manuscripts Commission. <u>Reports</u>. Series 1-81, 1870-1946. Washington, D.C., 1962.

   OGU mcd   OOU mfe (LP)

   Guides: Great Britain. Historical Manuscripts Commission. <u>Guide to the Reports of the Royal Commission on Historical Manuscripts, 1870-1911</u>. London, H.M.S.O., 1914.

   Great Britain. Historical Manuscripts Commission. <u>Guide to the Reports of the Royal Commission on Historical Manuscripts, 1911-1957</u>. 3 vols. London, H.M.S.O. 1966-

   Great Britain. Historical Manuscripts Commission, <u>Publications of the Royal Commission on Historical Manuscripts, Revised to 31st August 1961</u>. Government Publications Sectional List, 24, London H.M.S.O., 1961. Washington, Microcard Editions, 1966.

257. Great Britain. Home Dept. <u>Correspondence H.O. 100/25-27</u>. London, Public Record Office, 1966. 2 reels.

   OTU mfm (LP)

258. Great Britain. Home Office. <u>Correspondence and Papers, Disturbances 1812-1855</u>. Toronto, Micromedia, 1977. 46 reels.

    OWL mfm (LP)

259. Great Britain. Laws Statutes, etc. <u>Statutes of the Realm (1225-1713)</u> 10v. and Index. Washington: Microcard Editions.

    OGU mcd   OSUL mcd (L)
    OOU mcd (LP)

260. Great Britain. Ministry of Munitions. <u>History of the Ministry of Munitions</u>. Hassocks, Sussex, Eng., Harvester Press.

    OHM mfe (LP)   OWTU mfe

261. Great Britain. Parliament. <u>Parliamentary Debates</u>. (Parliamentary History of England from 1066-1803., by William Cobbett.) New York, Microprint.

    OGU mpt   OOCC mpt

262. Great Britain. Parliament. <u>The Parliamentary Debates, 1803-1908</u>. New York, Readex Microprint.

    OGU mpt   OPET mcd (1830-90) (L)
    OOCC mpt

263. Great Britain. Parliament. <u>Parliamentary Debates, 1909-18</u>. New York, Readex Microprint.

    OGU mpt   OOCC mpt

264. Great Britain. Parliament. House of Commons. <u>British Sessional Papers, 1731-1800</u>. (The Abbot Collection) New York, Readex Microprint Corp., 1960.

    OGU mpt   OLU mpt (L)   OTU mpt
    OHM mpt (L)   OOCC mpt   OTY mpt
    OKQ mpt (L)   OPET mpt (L)   QMM mpt

    Guides: Gt. Brit. Parliament. House of Commons. <u>Hansard's Catalogue and Breviate of Parliamentary Papers, 1696-1834</u>. Reprinted in Facsimile with an Introduction by P. Ford and G. Ford. Oxford, Blackwell, 1953.

264. (Cont'd)

Gt. Brit. Parliament. House of Commons. List of House of Commons Sessional Papers, 1701-1750. Edited by Sheila Lambert. London, Swift (P&D) Distributed to Subscribers, 1968.

Gt. Brit. Parliament. House of Commons. Sessional Papers of the Eighteenth Century 1761-1800, Edited by Sheila Lambert. 2 vols. Wilmington Delaware, Scholarly Resources, Inc., 1976.

265. Great Britain. Parliament. House of Commons. British Sessional Papers, 1802-1900. New York. Readex Microprint Corp. 1942?-1960.

OGU	mpt		OPET	mpt	(L)
OHM	mpt	(L)	OTU	mpt	
OKQ	mpt	(L)	OTY	mpt	
OLU	mpt	(LP)	OWTU	mpt	
OOCC	mpt		QMM	mpt	

Guides: British Parliamentary Papers. General Index 1801-1899. Shannon, Ireland Irish University Press.

Ford, Percy. Select List of British Parliamentary Papers, 1833-1899, by P. Ford and G. Ford. Oxford, Blackwell, 1953.

Jones, Hilda V. Catalogue of Parliamentary Papers, 1801-1900, with a Few of Earlier Date. London, P.S. King, 1904.

266. Great Britain. Parliament. House of Commons. British Sessional Papers, 1901-   New York, Readex Microprint Corp., 1968?

OGU	mpt	(1901-1972-	)		OTU	mpt	(1901-)
OKQ	mpt	(1901-1930)	(L)		QMM	mpt	(1901-1908)
OLU	mpt	(1901-1970-	)	(LP)			

Guides: Ford, Percy and Ford, Grace Lister. A Breviate of Parliamentary Papers, 1900-1916, 1917-1939 and 1940-1954. Oxford etc., Blackwell, 1957-61.

Ford Percy. A Guide to Parliamentary Papers, What They are, How to Find Them, by P. Ford and G. Ford. 3rd ed. Totowa, N.J., Rowman and Littlefield, 1972.

Gt. Brit. Parliament. House of Commons. British Sessional Papers, Collection of Indexes, 1696-1900. New York, Readex Microprint Corp. 1964.

Gt. Brit. Parliament. House of Commons. General Index to the Bills, Reports and Papers Printed by Order of the House of Commons and to the Reports and Papers Presented by Command, 1900-1948-49. London, H.M. Stationary off., 1960.

267. Great Britain. Parliament. House of Commons. <u>Journals 1547-1900</u>.
New York, Readex Microprint Corp.

    OLU mpt (LP)   QMM mpt

268. Great Britain. Parliament. House of Commons. <u>Reports from Committees of the House of Commons 1715-1801.</u> Printed But not Inserted in the Journals of the House, with Printed Index. London, Chadwyck-Healey, 1973.

    OLU mfm (LP)   OOCC mfm (P)

    Guide: Gt. Brit. Parliament. House of Commons. <u>General Index to the Reports from Committees of the House of Commons 1715-1801</u>. Bishops Stortford, Herts., Chadwyck-Healey Ltd., 1973.

269. Great Britain. Parliament. House of Lords. <u>Sessional Papers. 1806-1859</u>. Bobbs Ferry, N.Y., Oceana Publications Inc., 1970.

    OTU mfm   QMM mfm (P)
    OWTU mfm (P)

    Guides: Great Britain. Parliament. House of Lords. <u>A General Index to the Sessional Papers Printed by Order of the House of Lords or Presented by Special Command...(1801-59)</u>. 1860. Reprint. Dobbs Ferry, N.Y.: Oceana, 1976.

    <u>House of Lords Sessional Papers 1806-1859</u>: Reel Guide to Microfilm Edition and Checklist of Papers. Dobbs Ferry, N.Y.: Oceana, 1974.

270. Great Britain. Privy Council. <u>Act of the Privy Council of England, v.1-43; 1542-1628.</u> Washington: Microcard Editions, 573 cards.

    OGU mcd   OSUL mfe (L)
    OOU mcd (L)

271. Great Britain. Privy Council. <u>Acts of the Privy Council of England, Colonial Series, 1613-1783.</u> Washington D.C., Microcard Editions, Microfiche/Microcard. 122 fiche.

    OGU mcd   QLB mfe (L)
    OOU mcd (L)

272. Great Britain. Privy Council. <u>Registers, 1631-37</u>. London, H.M.S.O., 1962. (Public Records Office P.C. 2/41-47) 200 cards.

    OGU mcd   OKQ mcd (L)

273. Great Britain. Public Record Office. <u>Calendar of Letters and State Papers, Foreign and Domestic. Henry VIII, 1509-1545.</u> 20 vols. Washington D.C., Microcard Editions. 610 fiche.

    OGU mfe   OWA mfe (L)
    OPET mcd (L)   QLB mfe (L)
    OSUL mfe (L)

274. Great Britain. Public Record Office. <u>Calendar of State Papers, 1202-1675.</u> (State papers and manuscripts relating to English affairs, existing in the archives and collections of Venice and other libraries of Northern Italy). Washington, D.C., Microcard Editions, 1968.

    OLU mfe (LP)   OSUL mfe (268 fiche) (L)

    Guide: Gt. Brit. Public Record Office. <u>Guide to the Contents of the Public Record Office.</u> vol.2, London, H.M.S.O., 1963.

275. Great Britain. Public Record Office. <u>Calendar of State Papers, Colonial Series, 1574-1733.</u> v.1-40. Washington., D.C., 1965. Microcard Editions. 602 fiche.

    OGU mcd   QLB mfe (L)
    OPET mcd (L)

276. Great Britain. Public Record Office. <u>Calendar of State Papers, Domestic Series, Charles I, 1625-1649.</u> 23 vols. Washington, D.C., Microcard Editions, 1964. 385 fiche.

    OGU mfe   QLB mfe (L)
    OPET mcd (L)

277. Great Britain. Public Record Office. <u>Calendar of State Papers Domestic Series, Charles II 1660-1670.</u> 18 v. Washington, D.C., Microcard Editions, 1967.

    OGU mfe

278. Great Britain. Public Record Office. <u>Calendar of State Papers, Domestic Series.</u> The Commonwealth, 1649-1660. 13 vols. Washington, D.C., Microcard Editions.

    OGU mfe   QLB mfe (L)
    OPET mcd (L)

279. Great Britain. Public Record Office. <u>Calendar of State Papers, Domestic Series. Edward VI, Mary, Elizabeth 1, 1547-1625.</u> 12 vols. Washington, D.C., Microcard Editions. 200 fiche.

    OGU mfe   OSUL mfe (L)
    OPET mcd (L)   QLB   mfe/mcd (L)

280. Great Britain. Public Record Office. <u>Calendar of State Papers, Domestic Series. William III, 1689-95.</u> 6 vols. Washington: Microcard Editions, 1967, Microfiche.

    OGU mfe

281. Great Britain. Public Record Office. <u>Calendar of State Papers, Foreign Series. Edward VI, 1547-1553; Mary, 1553-1558; Elizabeth 1, 1558-1582.</u> 18 vols. Washington, D.C., 1964. Microcard Editions. 278 fiche.

    OGU mfe   OSUL mfe (L)
    OPET mfe (L)   QLB   mfe (L)

282. Great Britain. Public Record Office. <u>Foreign Office Records and Consular Reports from the Ottoman Empire.</u> n.p., n.d. London, Public Record Office. (Publication no. FO78) 6 reels.

    QMM mfm (P)

283. Great Britain. Public Record Office. <u>F.O. Registers: China, 1865-1915 Coolie Emigration.</u> London, Public Record Office, 1965- 8 reels.

    OTU mfm (LP)

284. Great Britain. Public Record Office. <u>MSS. Calendar and indexes to the Patent Rolls, 1 Elizabeth 1-7 William IV.</u> (n.p., 1558-1837) London, Public Record Office. 15 reels.

    OTU mfm (LP)

285. Great Britain. Public Record Office. <u>Rerum Britannicarum Medii Revi Scriptores.</u> Chronicles and Memorials of Great Britain and Ireland During the Middle Ages. Washington, D.C., Microcard Editions. Also Known as Rolls Series. Microcard.

    OGU mcd (nos. 1-99)   OSTCB mcd (nos.1-13, 23, 57)
    OPET mfe (nos. 1-99) (L)   (L)

286. Great Britain. Public Record Office. Royal Air Force: Final Reports on Operations - Night Raids, Feb. 1942-May 1945. Wilmington, Scholarly Resources, Inc. 5 reels.

   OHM   mfm   (LP)

287. Great Britain. Public Record Office. Treasury Minute Books, 1719-22 and 1725-28. London, H.M.S.O., 1962. 24 cards.

   OKQ   mcd   (L)

288. Great Britain. Public Record Office. Unpublished State Papers of English Civil War and Interregnum, Hassocks, Sussex, Eng., Havester Press.

   OHM   (Part 1,2,4)   mfm   (LP)

289. Great Britain. Registrar General. Statistical Review of England and Wales. 45 v., 1921-65. N.J., Somerset House. 1974. 16 reels.

   OHM   mfm   (LP)   OWTU   mfm

290. Great Britain. Treasury Solicitor. The 1745 Rebellion Papers, 1745-1753. Toronto, Micromedia, 1977. 8 reels.

   OWL   mfm   (L)

291. Grimes, Louis Arthur. The Collection of the Honourable Louis Arthur Grimes, 1883-1948. (Liberian pamphlets, orations, documents and newspapers) Bedford, N.Y.: African Imprint Library Services, 1973. 6 reels.

   QMG   mfm   (L)

292. Gul'binskii, Ignatii Vladislavovich. Literatura Velikogo Desiatiletii 1917-1927, Moskva. Tumba, Sweden. International Documentation Centre, 1965. Microfiche.

   QMM   mfe   (P)

293. Hague. Gemeentemuseum. Muziekbibliotheek. Collection Music Department Haags Gemeentemuseum, The Hague, Netherlands. Zug, Switz., Inter-Documentation Co., AG, 1972. 44 fiche.

   OWA   mfe   (LP)

294. Haïti. (Republic) Le Moniteur, <u>Journal Officiel de la République D'Haïti</u>, 1849-1906, 1916-1956, 1967-1968. N.Y., KTO Microform. 16 reels.

   OWTU mfm

295. Hakluyt, Richard. <u>The Principal Navigations, Voyages, Traffiques, and Discoveries of the English Nation</u>. London, Hakluyt Society, Microcard ed. by Micro Methods Ltd.

   OTR mfe (L)

296. Hakluyt Society. <u>Extra Series, v.1-12</u>. Wakefield, Eng., E.P. Microform Ltd.

   OTR mfe (L)

297. Hardy, Thomas. <u>Jude the Obscure; Original MS. From Fitzwilliam Museum, Cambridge</u>. East Ardsley, Wakefield, Yorks., Micro Methods Ltd. 1 reel.

   OTR mfm (L)

298. Hardy, Thomas. <u>The Original Manuscripts and Papers of Thomas Hardy</u>. Wakefield, Eng., E.P. Microform Ltd., 1975. 18 reels.

   OHM mfm (LP)   OWA mfm (LP)

299. <u>The Harleian Miscellany: or a Collection of Scarce, Curious and Entertaining Pamphlets and Tracts, as Well in Manuscript, as in Print, Found in the Late Earl of Oxford's Library. 1808-11</u>. 12 vols. vol. 12 is Index. Louisville, Ky: Lost Cause Press. 153 cards.

   OGU mcd

300. Henry Bradshaw Society, London. <u>Publications</u>. 1891-   New York, Microcard Editions.

   OWA mfe (LP)

301. <u>Henry Knox Papers, 1719-1825</u>. Boston, Massachusetts Historical Society, 1960.

   OLU mfm (LP)

301.   (Cont'd)

   Guide: Index to the Henry Knox Papers Owned by the New England Historic Geneological Society and Deposited in the Massachusetts Historical Society. Boston, Mass., Massachusetts Historical Society, 1960.

302. Herodotus. Historiae. East Ardsley, Wakefield, York, Micro Methods Ltd., 1 reel.

   OTR   mfm   (L)

303. Herstory. Selected Periodicals and Newspapers at the Women's History. Research Center Library, Berkeley, Calif. Wooster, Ohio: Bell and Howell, 1972. 23 reels.

   OWTU   mfm   (LP)   QMG   mfm   (L)

   Guides: Herstory Microfilm Collection: Table of Contents. Berkeley, Calif.: Women's History Library, 1972.

   Reel Guide to Herstory Supplementary Set 1: Herstory 1 Addenda: Herstory 1 Update: Herstory 2: And Title Index to Supplementary Sets 1 & 2: Microfilm Edition of the International Women's History Periodical Archive. Berkeley, Calif.: Women's History Research Center, 1976.

   Reel Guide to Herstory Supplementary Set 2: Herstory 1 Continuing Update: Herstory 2 Update: Herstory 3. Berkeley, Calif.: Women's History Research Center, 1976.

304. Hillquit, Morris, 1869-1933. The Morris Hillquit Papers. Madison, Madison, State Historical Society of Wisconsin, 1969? 10 reels.

   QMG   mfm   (L)

305. Hispanic Culture Series. n.p., Louisville, Ky., University of Kentucky Libraries Microfilm Center, 1965-1969. 333 reels.

   OTU   mfm   (LP)

   Guides: British Museum. Dept. of Printed Books. Short-Title Catalogue of Books Printed in Spain and of Spanish Books Printed Elsewhere in Europe Before 1601 now in the British Museum, London. Printed by Order of the Trustees, 1921.

   Hispanic Society of America, Library. List of Books Printed Before 1601 in the Library of the Hispanic Society of America, by Clara Louisa Penney. New York, Printed by Order of Trustees, the Hispanic Society of America, 1955.

305.   (Cont'd)

   Simon Diaz, J. <u>Bibliografia de Literatura Hispanica Madrid</u>, Consejo Superior de Investigaciones Cientificas Instituto, Miguel de Cervantes de Filologia Hispanica, 1950-72.

306. Historical Tracts, a Gift of Mrs. Peter Redpath to the Redpath Library, McGill University, Montreal (v.p.) 1754-1800. Montreal, McGill University Library Photoduplication Service, 1964.

   OTU mfm v.277-445, 448-576 (LP)   QMM mfm (P)

   Guide: McGill University, Montreal. Library. <u>Catalogue of a Collection of Historical Tracts, 1561-1800, in 582 v.</u> London, Printed by the Donor, 1901.

307. <u>The History of Women</u>. A Comprehensive Collection Based on the Holdings of Nine Major Libraries. New Haven, Research Pub'ns, 1976.

   OWTU mfm (LP)

308. Holyoake Papers, 1831-1905, From the Collection in the Bishopgate Institute, London, England. East Ardsley, Wakefield, York., Micro Methods, 1972. 28 reels.

   OHM mfm (LP)   QMM mfm (P)

309. Holyoake Papers, 1840-1906, From the Collection in the Co-operative Union Library. East Ardsley, Wakefield, Yorks., Micro Methods, 1972. Microfilm.

   OHM mfm (LP)   QMM mfm (P)

310. Howell, George. Selected Items From the George Howell Collection at the Bishopsgate Institute, London. East Ardsley, Wakefield, Yorks, Micro Methods, 1964. 25 reels.

   OHM mfm (LP)   QMM mfm (P)
   QMG mfm (L)

311. Huegel, Friedrich. Freiherr von. <u>Diaries, 1877-1924</u>. Chicago, Joseph Regenstein Library, University of Chicago, 1967. 11 reels.

   OWL mfm (LP))

312. The Human Environment Microlibrary. -- New York: Microfiche Publications, 1973. (The full text of reports and documents on international environmental affairs including the U.N..Conference on the Human Environment, Stockholm, 1972.) 906 fiche.

    OGU mfe   OLU mfe (LP)
    OHM mfe   OTU mfe (LP)

    Guide: The Human Environment. Washington, D.C., Woodrow Wilson International Center for Scholars, 1972.

313. Human Relations Area Files. New Haven, Conn., H.R.A.F. Press. University Microfilms 1958-

    OGU mfe   OPAL mfe (LP)
    OHM mfe (LP)   OTU   mfe (LP)
    OKQ mfe (v.1-4) (LP)   OWTU mfe (L)
    OLU mfe (LP   QQLA mfe (L)
    OOCC mfe

    Guides: Behavioural Science Notes. New Haven, Conn., HRAF, Inc., v v.1. 1966.

        Human Relations Area Files, Inc. Bibliography of Sources Processed for the Files. Rev. (compiled by John M. Beierle) New Haven, Conn., HRAF, Inc., 1961.

        Human Relations Area Files Inc. HRAF Source Bibliography. (compiled by Joan Steffens and Timothy J. O'Leary) New Haven, Conn., H.R.A.F., Inc., 1969.

        Human Relations Area Files, Inc. Outline of Cultural Materials (by George P. Murdock and others) 4th ed. Rev. New Haven, Conn., HRAF., Inc., 1961.

        Murdock, George P. Ethnographic Atlas. Pittsburg, University of Pittsburg Press, 1967.

        Murdock, George P. Outline of World Cultures, 2nd ed., Rev. New Haven, Conn., HRAF, Inc., 1958.

314. Hungary. Ministry of Foreign Affairs. Hungarian Peace Negotiations, v.1, 1920. Ann Arbor, Mich., University Microfilms.

    OHM mfm (LP)

315. Imperial Gazetteers of India. India Gazetteers; Provincial (Series) 19v. Zug, Switzerland, Inter Documentation, Co., 1973-

    OTU mfe (LP)

316. <u>Imperial Gazetteers of India</u>. <u>India Gazetteers; District (Series)</u>,
v.1-122. Zug, Switzerland, Inter Documentation, Co., 1973-

    OTU mfe (LP)

317. India. Legislature. Legislative Council. <u>Abstracts of the Proceedings of the Council of the Governor-General of India Assembled for the Purpose of Making Laws and Regulations</u>. Calcutta, 1863. Tumba, Sweden, International Documentation Centre.

    QMM mfe (1862-1920) (P)

318. India. Legislature. Legislative Council. <u>Proceedings of the Legislative Council of India Calcutta, 1856-</u>   Tumba, Sweden International Documentation Centre.

    QMM mfe (1856-1861) (P)

319. India. Linguistic Survey. <u>Linguistic Survey of India</u>. Culcutta, Office of the Superintendent of Government Printing, 1903-29? Tumba, Sweden, International Documentation Centre.

    QMM mfe (P)

320. India Census Commissioner. <u>Census of India 1871/72-1951</u>. Zug, Switzerland, Inter-Documentation Co., 1966-

    OGU mfe   OTU mfe

    Guide: <u>India Census, 1872-1951. A Checklist and Index</u>. Zug, Switzerland, Inter-Documentation Company, 1966.

321. Informatech France-Quebec. <u>Bulletin Référence 83</u> (Urbanisme-Environment) Montréal, Informatech France-Quebec, 1972-

    OOU mfe (LP)

    Guide: Reference 83: Index des Descripteurs.

322. Institut Canadien du Film/Canadian Film Institute. <u>Documentation Filmographique/Film Title Index</u>. Canadian Film Institute, 1970?

    OOU mfm (LP)

323. Institute of Chartered Accountants in England and Wales. London. <u>Microfilmed Collection of Rare Books on Accounting and Related Subjects, 15th-19th Centuries</u>. Selected and Arranged for the Institute, by B.S. Yamey. London, World Microfilms Publications, 1970.

    OWA mfm 30 reels (LP)   QMG mfm 11 reels (L)

    Guides: The Institute of Chartered Accountants: <u>Microfilmed Collection of Rare Books on Accounting and Related Subjects: Complete List of Titles and Index to Contents by Reel</u>. 2d ed. London: World Microfilms, 1971.

    Paul, Geoffrey. <u>Historical Accounting Literature: A Catalogue of the Collection of Early Works on Bookkeeping and Accounting in the Library of the Institute of Chartered Accountants in England and Wales, Together with a Bibliography of Literature on the Subject Published Before 1750 and Not in the Institute Library</u>. London: Mansell, 1975.

324. <u>International Population Census Publication, Series 1, 1945-1967</u>. Woodbridge, Research Publication, Inc., 1976-77. (not including Canada, U.S. and India)

    OTU mfm (P)   QMM mfm (P)

325. <u>International Population Census Publication, Series II, 1945-1967</u>. Woodbridge, Conn., Research Publications, Inc.

    OTU mfm (P)   OWTU mfm (LP)

    Guide: <u>Bibliography and Reel Index. A Guide to the Microfilm Edition of International Population Census Publications 1945-67</u>. 4 vols. in 1. Woodbridge, Conn., Research Publications 1976.

326. Isaac Hobhouse and Co. <u>The Hobhouse Letters, 1722-1755; Letters and Other Papers of Isaac Hobhouse and Co.</u>, Bristol Merchants. Introd. by Walter Minchinton. East Ardsley, Eng., Micro Methods, 1963. (Recieved as part of British records relating to America in microform)

    OTU mfm

327. <u>Italian Books Before 1601</u>. Lexington, Ky., Erasmus Press, 1965-

    OGU mfm   OTU mfm (LP)
    OLU mfm (LP)

327.   (Cont'd)

   Guides: Italian Books Before 1601. Index. (Lexington, Ky., Erasmus Press,) 1965-

   British Museum. Dept. of Printed Books. Short-Title Catalogue of Books Printed in Other Countries from 1465-1600 now in the British Museum. London, Trustees of the British Museum, 1958.

   Short-Title Catalogue of Books Printed in Italy and of Books Printed Abroad 1501-1600. Boston, Mass., G.K. Hall & Co., 1970.

328. Italian Drama on Microfilm. (v.p., v.d.,) Lexington, Ky., Erasmus Press, 1967-74.

   OGU mfm   OTU mfm (LP)

   Guides: Clubb, Louise George. Italian Plays (1500-1700) in the Folger Library: A Bibliography with Introduction. Florence: Olschki, 1968.

   Corrigan, Beatrice. Catalogue of Italian Plays 1500-1700 in the Library of the University of Toronto. Toronto: University of Toronto Press, 1961.

   Herrick, Marvin Theodore. Italian Plays 1500-1700 in the University of Illinois Library. Urbana: University of Illinois Press, 1966.

329. Italy. Foreign Office. The Sonnino Papers, Nov., 1914-June 1919. Ann Arbor, Mich., University Microfilms. 54 reels.

   OHM mfm (LP)

330. Jamaica. Assembly. Journals, 1663-1826. Wilmington, Scholarly Resources, Inc.

   OWTU mfe

331. Japanese Monographs. Washington, Library of Congress Microfilming Unit Microfilm. "A collection of historical studies on the war in the Pacific during World War II, originally prepared by former officers of the imperial Japanese Army and Navy, and edited by the Far East Command, Military History Section, Dept. of the Army". Includes Japanese Studies on Manchuria and Japanese Night Combat Study.

   OTU mfm (LP)

331.   (Cont'd)

   Guide: U.S. Dept. of the Army. Office of Military History. Guide to Japanese Monographs and Japanese Studies of Manchuria, 1945-1960. Washington, 196   Washington, D.C., Library of Congress Photoduplication Service, 1971.

332. Japanese Relocation Camp and Assembly Center Newspapers. Washington: Library of Congress Photoduplication Service and Serial Division, 1977. 22 reels.

   OGU mfm

333. Jayakar, Mukund Ramrao. Jayakar Papers. New Delhi, National Archives of India, 1970. 10 reels.

   OTU mfm (LP)

334. Jefferson, Thomas. The Writings of Thomas Jefferson With a Comprehensive Analytical Index. 20 v. 1905. Cleveland. Micro Photo Division, Bell and Howell Co., n.d. 5 reels.

   OWA mfm (LP)

335. Jeffersonian Americana from the University of Virginia Library. (v.p., v.d.) Washington, D.C., Microcard Editions, Inc., 1955. 2000 fiche.

   OTU mfe (LP)

   Guides: Jeffersonian Americana from the University of Virginia Library. Washington, D.C., Microcard Editions, 1965.

   Sabin, Joseph. Bibliotheca Americana: A Dictionary of Books Relating to America from its Discovery to the Present Time. 29 vols. 1868-1936. Reprint. Metuchen, N.J., Scarecrow, 1966.

336. The Jesuit Relations and Allied Documents. Edited by Reuben Gold Thwaites. 1896-1901. 73 vols. Washington, D.C., Microcard Editions. 276 cards.
   "Travels and explorations of the Jesuit missionaries in New France, 1610-1791, in the original French, Latin, and Italian texts, with English translations and notes".

   OPAL mcd (L)

337. **Journaux, Période de la Commune.** Paris, Association pour la Conservation et la Reproduction Photographique de la Presse, 1967-69. 4 reels.
"Microfilm of the Paris newspapers made from the originals in the Bibliothèque nationale, Paris."

   OTU mfm (LP)

338. K'ang Jih Chan-Cheng Tzu-Liao (1) Arlington, Va., Cooper-Trent Division/Keuffel and Esser, 1970. 7 reels.

   QMM mfm (P)

339. **Kentucky Culture**, 2277 vols. Louisville, Ky. Lost Cause Press.

   OGU mcd   OLU mcd (LP)

   Guide: Coleman, J.W. **A Bibliography of Kentucky History**. Lexington, University of Kentucky Press, 1949.

340. **Kentucky Microcard Series.** Lexington, University of Kentucky Press. 1968?
   Important original studies not suitable for letterpress publication. Series B: Library Science.

   OTU mcd (P)

341. King, William Lyon Mackenzie. **Mackenzie King Diaries, 1893-1931**. Toronto, University of Toronto Press, 1973. (Index provide by University of Toronto Press.)

   OGU mfe   OTU mfe (LP)
   OOU mfe (LP)   OWA mfe (L)
   OPAL mfe (L)   OWL mfe (L)
   OSTCB mfe (L)   QMG mfe (L)

342. Ku, Ssu-Li (comp.) **Huang Ming Wen Hai**. Tokyo. Yushodo Microfilms 1963. 24 reels.
   "Manuscripts in 175 vols. in custody of Hosokawa family, formerly feudal lords of Kumamoto".

   OTU mfm (LP)

343. Laborde, Jean Benjamin de. Essai sur la Musique Ancienne et Moderne. Paris, 1780. 4 vols. Rochester, Rochester University Press. 58 cards.

    QMM mcd (P)

344. Labour Party (Great Britain). Report of the Annual Conference 1901-1973. Wakefield, Eng., EP Microform Ltd.

    OLU mfm (LP)

345. Labour Party (Great Britain) Executive Committee. National Executive Committee Minutes of the British Labour Party, 1900-1951. Hassocks, Sussex, Eng., Harvester Press, 1975.

    OLU mfe (1900-1951) (LP)   OPAL mfe (1900-1939) 266 fiche (L)

346. Labour Research Department. London. Books and Pamphlets, 1916-72 and Continuation. (with printed index) London: World Microfilm Publications, 1974. 9 reels.

    QMM mfm (P)

347. Labour Union Constitutions and Proceedings, 1836-1974. Glen Rock, N.J., Microfilming Corporation of America, 1975-

    QMG mfm Part 1 (L)

348. Lafontaine, Sir Louis Hippolyte Bart. Collection Lafontaine. (from the collection of the Société Historique de Montréal) Ottawa, Public Archives of Canada, 1966. 9 reels.

    OHM mfm (LP)   OWA   mfm (LP)
    OPAL mfm (LP)   QSHERU mfm (L)
    OTU mfm (LP)

349. Lambeth Palace Library. The Fulham Papers. With Printed Index. London, World Microfilms Publication. 1970. 19 reels.

    OHM mfm (LP)
    OOU mfm (LP)
    QMM mfm (P) (reels 1,11,17,18, and 19 containing Canadian material)

    Guide: Manross, William Wilson. The Fulham Papers in Lambeth Palace Library; American Colonial Section Calendar and Indexes. Oxford, Clarendon Press, 1965.

350. Lambeth Palace, Library. <u>Registers of the Archbishops of Canterbury, 13-17th Centuries</u>. With printed index. London, World Microfilms Publications.

    QMM mfm (P)

351. <u>Landmarks of Science; a Comprehensive Collection of the Source Materials in the History of Science</u>. New York, Readex Microprint Corp., 1967-

    OGU mpt   OTY mpt
    OLU mpt (L)   QMM mpt
    OTU mpt (LP)

352. <u>Latin American Documents</u>. Lexington, Erasmus Press, 1960-   Cambridge, Mass., General Microfilm Company. Project A: Recent Books; Project B: Documents and Uncopyrighted Current Books.

    OGU mcd 1960   OGU mfm 1969

    Guide: <u>Inter-American Review of Bibliography</u>. 1, 1951-   Washington, Pan American Union. 'Recent Books' Section (for project A)

353. Laurendeau, André. <u>Collection D'Articles de M. André Laurendeau Parus dans le Devoir 1947-1967</u>. -- Montréal: Société Canadienne du Microfilm, 1975? 2 reels.

    OTU mfm (LP)

354. Laurier, Sir Wilfrid. <u>The Laurier Papers</u>. Series A,B,C,D. Canada, Public Archives. 206 reels.

    OKQ mfm (L)

    Guide: Canada. Public Archives. <u>The Laurier Papers</u>: Author Index; Subject Index.

355. League of Nations. <u>Armaments Yearbook</u>. Category IX. 1924-1940. New Haven, Conn., Research Publications, Inc.

    OLU mfm (LP)

356. League of Nations. <u>Assembly Documents, 1919-1946</u>. New Haven, Conn., Research Publications.

    OLU mfm (LP)

357. League of Nations. Circular Letters from the Secretary General, 1919-1946. New Haven, Conn., Research Publications.

   OLU   mfm   (LP)

358. League of Nations, Council Documents, 1919-1946. New Haven, Conn., Research Publications.

   OLU   mfm   (LP)

359. League of Nations. Documents and Publications, 1919-1946. New Haven, Conn., Research Publications Inc.

   OLU   mfm   (LP)

360. League of Nations. Mandate Reports. Listed by Mandatory Power. New Haven, Conn., Research Publications, Inc.

   OLU   mfm   (LP)

361. League of Nations. Official Journal (records of the Assembly, and the minutes of the Council). New Haven, Conn., Research Publications, Inc.

   OOCC mfe   (Records of Assembly, 1919-46) (P)
   OOCC mfm   (The minutes of the Council, 1919-1940) (P)

362. League of Nations. Review of World Trade 1910-1936. New Haven, Conn., Research Publications, Inc.

   OLU   mfm   (LP)

363. League of Nations. Treaty Series, 1919-1947. v.1-205. New Haven, Conn., Reseach Publications Inc.

   OLU   mfm   (LP)

   Guides: Reel Indexes: vol. 1-63 on reel 71, vol. 64-130 on reel 72, vol. 131-193 on reel 73, vol. 194-205 on reel 74.

   Rohn, Peter H. World Treaty Index. Santa Barbara, Calif., American Bibliographical Centre-Clio Press, 1974.

364. The Left in Britain. Hassocks, Sussex, Harvester Press, 1974-
(Harvester Primary Sources Series)   124 fiche.

   OKQ   mfe   (LP)

365. Lewis, John Llewellyn, 1880-1969. The John L. Lewis Papers, 1879-1969.
Madison, Wis., State Historical Society of Wisconsin, 1970.   4 reels.

   QMG   mfm   (L)

366. Library Science Research Studies. nos. 1-   Rochester, N.Y., Univ. of
Rochester Press, 1960-   ; Washington, Microcard Editions Sponsored by Assoc. of College and Research Libraries to Disseminate
'Reports, Studies, etc. resulting from research in fields of library
and information science and historical descriptive and enumerative
bibliography'.

   OTU   mcd   (L)

367. Lincoln Record Society. Publications. v.1-50, (1910/11-1956). Bishop's
Stortford, England, Chadwyck - Healey.   213 fiche.

   OKQ   mfe   (LP)

368. Literature of Theology and Church History. Louisville, Kentucky, Lost
Cause Press, 1976.

   OWL   mfe   (L)

369. Liverpool Papers. American Material in the Liverpool Papers, 1727-1828;
a Section of Material Relating to the American Colonies and the
United States from Liverpool Papers in the British Museum, London.
East Ardsley, Wakefield, Eng., Micro Methods, 1965.
(Recieved as part of British records relating to America in micro-
form)

   OHM   mfm   (LP)

370. London. Stationer's Company. Records. Ann Arbor, Mich., University
Microfilms, 1953.   29 reels.

   OKQ   mfm   29 reels   (LP)   OTU   mfm   (LP)

371. London Directories from the Guildhall Library, 1677-1900. Wakefield,
Yorks, EP Microform, 1972?   22 reels.

   QMG   mfm   Group 1, 1677-1799   (L)

371.   (Cont'd)

   Guide: Goss, Charles W.F. The London Directories 1677 to 1855: A Bibliography with Notes on Their Origin and Development. London: D. Archer, 1932.

372. London Trades Council. Minutes and Papers, 1860-1953. London, World Microfilms, 1972. 11 reels.

   OSUL mfm (LP)   QMM mfm (P)

373. Losely Manuscripts: Manuscripts of the Revels Office in the Time of Henry VIII, Edward VI and Mary, Ca. 1540-1580. s.l., s.n. 2 reels.

   OKQ mfm (LP)

374. Mackenzie Valley Pipeline Inquiry. Briefs and Transcripts of Public Hearings. Toronto, Micromedia Ltd., 1975.

   OLU   mfm (LP)   OPET mfm (LP)
   OOCC mfm (P)   OTU   mfm

   Guides: Mackenzie Valley Pipeline Inquiry. Index to Briefs and Transcripts. Toronto, Micromedia, Ltd., 1975.

   Mackenzie Valley Pipeline Inquiry. Index to Transcripts and Exhibits, Toronto, Micromedia, Ltd., 1975-

375. Maclean Hunter Microfilm Services. Lester B. Pearson 1897-1972. Toronto, Maclean Hunter Microfilm Services, 1972. 11 fiche.

   OTU mfe (LP)

376. MacLeod, Roy M. & James R. Friday. Archives of British Men of Science: a Survey of Private and Institutional Holdings of British Scientific Archives. London: Mansell, c1972. 58 fiche.

   QMM mfe (P)

377. Les Maîtres Musiciens de la Renaissance Française. Editions publiées par n. Henry Expert. Sur les manuscrits les plus authentiques et les meilleurs imprimes du XVIe siècle, avec variantes, notes historiques et critiques, transcriptions en notation moderne, etc. Paris, A. Leduc, 1894-1908. 23 vols. (Plus bibliographie the matique). New York University Music Editions Inc., 1973.

   OWA mfe 61 cards (L)

378. Manitoba. <u>Manitoba Gazette, 1870-</u>   . Ottawa, Canadian Library
     Association.

   OGU mfm (1870-1900)   OPET mfm (1870-1900) (LP)

379. Manitoba. Laws, Statutes, etc. <u>Manitoba Statutes</u>. Ottawa, Canadian
     Library Association.

   OGU mfm (1876-1900, Revised statutes, 1891-1902)
   OSUL mfm (1871-1900) (LP)

380. Manitoba. Legislative Assembly. <u>Journals, 1870-1900</u>. Ottawa,
     Canadian Library Association.

   OGU mfm (1878-1890)   OTY   mfm (1871-1900)
   OPET mfm (1870-1900) (LP)

381. Manitoba. Legislative Council. <u>Journal, 1871-1876</u>. Ottawa, Canadian
     Library Association.

   OGU mfm (1871-1876)   OTY   mfm (1871-1876)
   OPET mfm (1871-1876)

382. Marpurg, Friedrich Wilhelm. <u>Historisch - Kritische Beytraege</u>, zur
     Aufnahme der Musik. 1754-1760. 5 vols. Rochester, Rochester
     University Press. 35 cards.

   QMM mcd (P)

383. Martens, George F. von, ed. <u>Nouveau Recueil de Traites D'Alliance,
     de Paix, de Trève, 1817-41</u>. 16 vols. Washington, D.C., Microcard
     Edition, 1964.

   QLB mcd (L)

384. Martens, George F. von, ed. <u>Nouveau Recueil Général de Traites,
     Conventions et Autres Transactions Remarquables, 1843-75</u>. 20 vols.
     Washington, D.C., Microcard Editions, 1964.

   QLB mcd (L)

385. Martens, George F. von, ed. <u>Nouveau Recueil Général de Traites et
     Autres Actes Relatifs aux Rapports de Droit International</u>.
     Washington, D.C., Microcard Editions, 1964.

   OOU mcd ser. 2, 1876-1908   (L)
   QLB mcd ser. 2, 1876-1908, ser. 3, 1908-1941   (L)

386. Martens, George F. von, ed. <u>Nouveau Supplément du Recueil de Traites</u>. Washington, D.C., Microcard Editions, 1964.

    QLB   mcd   3v. 1839-1842   (L)

387. Martens, George F. von, ed. <u>Recueil de Traites D'Alliance, de Paix de Trêve, 1817-1835</u>. Washington, D.C., Microcard Editions, 1964.

    OOU   mcd   (L)   QLB   mcd   (L)

388. Martens, George F. von, ed. <u>Supplément au Recueil des Principaux Traites D'Alliance de Paix, de Treve, 1802-1808</u>. Washington, D.C., Microcard Editions, 1964.

    OOU   mcd   (L)   QLB   mcd   (L)

389. Martens, George F. von, ed. <u>Table Général du Recueil des Traites, 1875-1876</u>. 2 vols. Washington, D.C., Microcard Editions.

    QLB   mcd   (L)

390. <u>Massachusetts Local Tax List Through 1776</u>. Waltham, Mass., Graphic Microfilm of New England. 25 reels.

    QMG   mfm   (L)

391. <u>Materialien zur Kunde des Aelteren Englischen Dramas</u>. 44 vols. 1902-1914. Washington: Microcard Editions. 237 fiche.

    OGU   mfe

392. Mather, Cotton, 1663-1728. <u>The Mather Papers</u>. Cambridge, Mass., Microreproduction Laboratory, M.I.T. Libraries, 1971? Part 1 19 reels.

    QMG   mfm   Part 1   (L)

393. Matsumoto, Tadao. Matsumoto Bunko. <u>Matsumoto Collection of the Press Cuttings Relating to China, the Early Twentieth Century</u>. Compiled by Matsumoto, Tadao, Tokyo, Yushodo.

    OTU   mfm   (LP)

394. <u>Menshevik Collection, 1903-19.</u> Stanford, Calif., Hoover Institution on War, Revolution and Peace. 49 reels. (In process)

    OOCC mfm (LP)

    Guides: <u>Menshevik Collection of Newspapers, Periodicals, Pamphlets and Books Related to the Menshevik Movement: Alphabetical Index.</u> Stanford, Hoover Institution on War, Revolution and Peace, Stanford University, 1967.

    <u>Menshevik Collection of Newspaper, Periodicals, Pamphlets and Books, Related to the Menshevik Movement: Reel Index.</u> Stanford, California: Hoover Institution on War, Revolution and Peace, Stanford University, 1967.

395. Metropolitan Toronto Central Library. <u>Biographical Scrapbooks.</u> Toronto, Microfilm Services, 1966. 32 reels.

    OHM mfm (LP)   OSUL mfm (LP)
    OGU mfm   QMG   mfe (L)
    OLU mfm (LP)

    Guide: Metropolitan Toronto Central Library. <u>Biographical Scrapbooks: Index.</u> Toronto, Metropolitan Toronto Library Board, 1973.

396. A Microform Library. <u>Sources for the History of Social Welfare in America.</u> Westport, Conn.: Microform Division, Greenwood Pub. Corp., 1970? 1638 fiche.

    OGU mfe

397. Migne, Jacques Paul. <u>Patrologiae Cursus Completus</u>: Series Graeca. Paris 1857-87. Washington, D.C., Microcard Foundation, 1961. 2607 fiche. (Text in Latin and Greek)

    OGU mcd   QMM mfe (P)
    OLU mcd

    Guides: Migne, Jacques Paul, ed. <u>J.P. Migne: Index Alphabeticus Omnium Doctorum-Patrum Scriptorumque Ecclesiasticorum Quorum Opera Scriptaque vel Minima in Patrologia Latina Reperiuntur. J.F. Pearson: Conspectus Auctorum Quorum Nomina Indicibus Patrologiae Graeco-Latinae a J.P. Migne Editae Continentur.</u> Ridgewood, N.J.: Gregg Press, 1965.

    Migne, Jacques Paul, ed. <u>Patrologiae Cursus Completus Accurante J.P. Migne. Series Graeca. Indices Digessit Ferdinand Cavallers.</u> Paris: Garnier, 1912.

397. (Cont'd)

Migne, Jacques Paul, ed. Patrologiae Cursus Completus. Series Graeca. Index Locupletissimus....... by Theodor Hopfner. Paris: P. Geuthner, 1928.

Peabody Institute. Baltimore. Library. Catalogue of the Library of the Peabody Institute of the City of Baltimore. Boston, G.K. Hall (1961). Part IV pp. 2908-12 (included in the collection) Provides Alphabetical Author Index to the Greek Series.

398. Migne, Jacques Paul. Patrologiae Cursus Completus: Series Latina. Paris, 1844-1882. Washington, D.C., Microcard Foundation, 1960. 3268 fiche.

```
OLU   mfe   (L)
OWA   mfe   (221 vols. 1844-1864)   (L)
OWL   mfe   (vols. 1-221, 1844-1864)
QMM   mfe   (P)
```

Guides: Migne, J.P. Patrologiae Cursus Completus. Series Latina. Indexes. Elucidatio in 235 Tabulas Patrologiae Latinae Auctore Cartusiensi. Series "Vox Romana". Rotterdam: Soc. Editr. De Forel, 1952.

Peabody Institute. Baltimore. Library. Catalogue of the Peabody Institute of the City of Baltimore. Boston, G.K. Hall (1961). Part 1-4, pp. 2913-27. (included in the collection provides alphabetical author index to the Latin series.)

Pearson, John Batteridge. A Complete List of the Names of the Authors Whose Works are Printed in the Greek Series of Migne's Patrologia. 1882. Reprint. Lexington, Mass.: Gregg International Publishers, North America, 1965.

Pearson, John Batteridge. Conspectus Auctorum Quorum Nomina Indicibus Patrologiae Graeco-Latinae a J.P. Migne Editae Continentur. Cambridge, England: Deighton, Bell, et Soc., 1882.

399. Missionary Periodicals from the China Mainland. Westport, Conn., Greenwood Press.

QMG   mfm   (L)

400. Montreal, Université de. Ecole de Bibliothécaires. <u>Bibliographies D'Auteurs Canadiens D'Expression Française</u>. 10 reels.

   OTU   mfm   (P)

   Guide: Laurin, Christiane. <u>Les Bio-Bibliographies et Bibliographies Compilées par les Étudiants de l'École des Bibliothécaires de l'Université de Montréal</u>: Liste et Index. Compilée par Mme Christiane Laurin sous la Direction de Jean-Pierre Chalifoux. Montréal Université de Montréal, 1970.

401. <u>Monumenta Germaniao Historica Inde ab Anno Christi Quingentesimo Usque ad Annum Millesimum et Quingentesimum</u>. Auctorum Antiquissimorunr t.1-15. Berolini, Apud Weidmannos, 1877-1919. Swedon, International Documentation Centre. 900 fiche.

   Qmm   mfe   (P)

402. Moravian Church of the American Indian Mission. <u>Missionary Records of Moravian Church of the American Indian Mission</u>. New Haven, Conn., Research Publications, Inc., 1970. Microfilm

   OLU   mfm   (LP)

   Guides: <u>Guide to the Records of the Moravian Mission Among the Indians of North America</u>. (reel guide) New Haven, Conn., Research Publications, Inc., 1970.

   Fliegel, Rev. Carl John. <u>Index to the Records of the Moravian Mission Among the Indians of North America</u>. New Haven, Conn., Research Publications, Inc., 1970.

403. Moscow, Publicahnaiă Biblioteka. <u>Eighteenth Century Russian Publications</u>. Cambridge, Mass., General Microfilm Co., 1968-   415 reels.

   QMM   mfm   (P)

404. <u>Musicache</u>. Editor: Lawson Cook. (Basic Music Library). Scarborough Ont., Berandol Music. Canada, Bell & Howell. 1002 fiche.

   QMM   mfe   (P)

   Guides: Cook, Lawson, ed. <u>Musicache: Index Fiche 1-1002</u>. Scarborough, Ont.: Berandol Music, n.d.

   Cook, Lawson, ed. <u>Musicache: Indexing System</u>. Scarborough, Ont., Berandol Music, n.d.

405. National Film Archive, London. <u>Film Title Index</u>. London, World
Microfilms, 1969. 43 reels.

    OOU mfm (LP)

406. Nationalsozialistische Deutsche Arbeiter Partei. Hauptarchiv. <u>NSDAP
Hauptarchiv</u> (Nazi Party archives) Stanford, Hoover Institution on
War, Peace and Revolution. 156 reels.
"Includes selected items from the Streicher and Himmler collections".

    OGU   mfm (selected titles)
    OHM   mfm reels 1-99, IA-55A, B (LP)
    OLU   mfm (LP)
    OTU   mfm (selected items (LP)
    OWTU mfm 1946-59 (LP)

    Guide: Heinz, G. <u>NSDAP Hauptarchiv</u>. Stanford, Hoover Institution
on War, Peace and Revolution, 1964. (Bibliographical series
17)

407. <u>New Hebrides Manuscripts on Microfilm</u>. Canberra: Pacific Manuscripts
Bureau, Australian National University, 197 -   . 15 reels.

    OHM mfm (LP)

408. <u>New York Times Oral History Program</u>. Glen Rock, N.J., Microfilm
Corporation of America, 1975.

    American Film Institute. <u>Edwin B. Hayes Oral History Collection</u>.
25 reels.

    <u>Columbia University Oral History Collection</u>. 45 reels.

    <u>Hebrew University Contemporary Jewry Oral History Collection</u>.

    <u>Stanford University Project South, Oral History Collection</u>. 2 reels.

    OHM mfm (LP)

    Guide: <u>The New York Times Oral History Program: Oral History Guide
no.1.</u>(Glen Rock, N.J.; Microfilming Corporation of America,
1976).

409. Newberry Library, Chicago. <u>Courtesy Books, 1571-1773</u>. (from collections in the Newberry Library) Wooster, Ohio. Microdivision,
Micro Photo Division, Bell & Howell. 19 reels.

    OGU   mfm   OMH mfm

409.   (Cont'd)

   Guide: Newberry Library, Chicago. <u>A Checklist of Courtesy Books in the Newberry Library.</u> Compiled by Virgil B. Heltzel. - Chicago, 1942. (on reel 1)

410. Newberry Library, Chicago. <u>French Political Pamphlets, 1560-1653, from Collections in the Newberry Library.</u> Wooster, Ohio, Micro Photo Division, Bell & Howell Co, 1970? 28 reels.

   OHM mfm (LP)   OTU mfm (LP)

   Guides: Newberry Library, Chicago. <u>A Checklist of French Political Pamphlets, 1560-1644 in the Newberry Library.</u> Compiled by Doris Varner Welsh, Chicago, Newberry Library.

   Newberry Library, Chicago. <u>A Second Checklist of French Political Pamphlets, 1560-1653, in the Newberry Library</u> Compiled by Doris Varner Welsh, Chicago, Newberry Library 1955.

411. Newfoundland. Legislative Assembly. <u>Journals, 1866-1900.</u> (b) <u>Statutes, 1866-1891.</u> CLA. Ottawa, Canadian Library Association.

   OGU mfm

412. <u>Northern Ireland Political Literature., Phase 1, 1968-72, Phase II, 1973-75. Collection in the Lindenhall Library, Belfast.</u> Dublin, Irish University Microforms. 218 cards.

   OGU mfe Phase 1   OWTU mfe Phase 1 (LP)
   OKQ mfe Phase 1 & 2 (LP)

   Guides: <u>Catalogue of Microfiche Series of Political Literature of Northern Ireland 1968-72</u>: Subject and Alphabetical Listings. Dublin: Irish Microforms, 1975.

   <u>Catalogue of Microfiche Series of Political Literature of Northern Ireland 1973-74 and 1975</u>: Subject and Alphabetical Listings. Dublin: Irish Microforms, 1977.

413. <u>Nottinghamshire Parish Registers: Marriages. 1898-1915.</u> Washington, D.C., Microcard Editions. 20 vols.

   OGU mcd

414. Obscestvennoe Dvizhenie v Rossii v Nachale XX-Veka. (pod red. IU. Martova ct dr.) Extended Micro Edition of International Documentation Centre AB. Tumba (Sweden), Hagelby House. 50 fiche.

    OPAL mfe (1909-1914) (L)

415. Odessa Miscellanea. Legal and Miscellaneous Papers. Odessa, 1807-77. London, Public Record Office.

    QSHERU mfm (L)

416. O'Donovan Rossa, Jeremiah. O'Donovan Rossa Papers. Washington, D.C., Catholic University of America, Dept. of Archives and Manuscripts, 1969?

    OWA mfm (LP)

417. Office des Communications Sociales, Montreal. Documentation Filmographique. Quebec, Bibliotheque Nationale de Quebec, 1970.

    OOU mfm (LP)

418. Ontario. Chief Election Officer. Return from the Records of the Legislative Assembly of the Province of Ontario, 1867-1975. Toronto, Ontario Election Office, 1972.

    OOU   mfm (1867-1975)   OSTCB mfm (1867-1975) (L)
    OPET   mfm (1867-1971) (L)   OTY   mfm (1867-1971)

419. Onatrio. Dept. of Crown Lands. Reports and Field Notes, (of surveyors) no.1-867 (includes Township plans), Scarborough, Ont., Standard Microfilm Reproductions Ltd.

    OOCC mfm (P)

420. Ontario. Dept. of Lands and Forests. Land Surveys Branch Record of Initial Land Surveys of Ontario, 8 parts. 185 reels.

    OLU mfm (LP)   OTY mfm (selected items)
    OKQ mfm (LP)

421. Ontario. Laws, Statutes, etc. Statutes of the Province of Ontario. v.1- , 1867- . Ottawa, Canadian Library Association.

    OGU mfm 1870-71, 1871-1897   OPET mfm 1869-1902 (LP)

422. Ontario. Legislative Assembly. <u>Debates 1867-1953</u>. Toronto, Ontario. Dept. of Public Records and Archives. Microfilm.

    OOCC mfm (P)   OTU mfm
    OSTCB mfm (1867-1946) (LP)   OTY mfm
    OSUL mfm (LP)

423. Ontario. Legislative Assembly. <u>Journal</u>. v.1- , 1867- . Ottawa, Canadian Library Association.

    OGU mfm (1867-1902)   OSUL mfm (1867-1902) (LP)
    OOCC mfm (1867-1902) (P)   OTY mfm (1874-1899)
    OPET mfm (1867-1902) (LP)

424. Ontario. Legislative Assembly. <u>Sessional Papers</u>. v.1-80, 1867/68-1948. Ottawa, Canadian Library Association.

    OGU mfm (1868-1902)   OSUL mfm (1868-1902)
    OOCC mfm (1868-1902) (LP)   OTY mfm (1868-1902)
    OPET mfm (1867-1948) (LP)

425. Organization of American States. <u>Actas de las Sessiones, 1945-1961</u>. Washington, D.C., Microcard Editions.

    OHM mfe (L)

426. Organization of American States. <u>Documentos Oficiales/Official Documents</u>. Washington, Microcard Editions, 1961-

    OHM mfe (1961-1970) (LP)   OTY mfe (1961-65, 1970)
    OOCC mfe (1961-1970) (LP)   OWTU mfe (P)
    OTU mfe

    Guide: Organization of American States. <u>Documentos Oficiales;
        Indice e Lista General</u>. Washington, D.C., Pan American Union. 1, 1960-

427. Organization of American States. Council. <u>Minutes of Meetings, 1948-1960</u>. Washington, D.C., Microcard Editions.

    OHM mfe (LP)

428. Owen, Robert. <u>Robert Owen Papers 1821-58</u>. Introduction by Peter d'A Jones. "Compiled from the original papers in the library of the Co-operative Union Ltd., Manchester". Wakefield, York, Micro Methods Ltd. 1 reel.

    OTR mfm (L)

429. Palais de Justice de Montreal. Archives. Recensement 1741 de la Compagnie des Indes. Montreal, Societe Canadienne du Microfilm, 1970. 1 reel.

   QSHERU mfm (L)

430. Pamiatniki Diplomaticheskikh Snosheniĭ Drevneĭ Rossii s Derzhavami Inostrannymi, 1851-1871. Sanktpeterburg. Tumba, Sweden, International Documentation Centre, 136 fiche.

   QMM mfe (P)

431. Pamphlets on Socialism, Communism, Bolshevism, etc., 1849-1931, Washington, D.C., Library of Congress Photoduplication Service, 1968. (In English, French or German) 3 reels.

   QMM mfm (P)

432. The Papers of William Penn. Philadelphia, Penn., The Historical Society of Pennsylvania, 1975.

   OLU mfm

   Guide: Guide to the Microfilm of the Papers of William Penn. Philadelphia, Penn., The Historical Society of Pennsylvania, 1975.

433. Papyrology on Microfiche, Ser.1. Missoula, Mo.: Published for the American Society of Papyrologists by Scholars Press, University of Montana, 1977.

   OHM mfe (LP)

434. Paris. Peace Conference, 1919. Select Reports of the American Commision to Negotiate the Peace. Arlington, Va., University Publications of America, 1976. 8 reels.

   OWL mfm (L)

435. Parker Society. Publications, v.1-55., 1849-1855. Louisville, Ky.: Lost Cause Press, 1957. 350 cards.

   OGU mcd

436. Partai Komunis Indonesia. Publications of the Communist Party of Indonesia, Djakarta, Pembarvan, 1945-1964. Zug, Switzerland, Inter Documentation, Co., 1969.

    OTU mfe (LP)   OWA mfe (L)

437. Peel Bibliography on Microfiche. Ottawa: National Library of Canada, 1975- (Microform copies of titles listed in Peel bibliography).

    OGU   mfe   OTU   mfe (LP)
    OHM   mfe (LP)   OTY   mfe
    OKQ   mfe (LP)   OWA   mfe (L)
    OOCC mfe (LP)   OWTU   mfe (L)
    OOU   mfe (LP)   QMM   mfe (P)
    OPAL mfe (L)   QSHERU mfe (L)
    OSUL mfe (L)

    Guides: Peel, Bruce Braden. A Bibliography of the Prairie Provinces to 1953. Toronto, University of Toronto Press, 1956.

        Peel, Bruce Braden. A Bibliography of the Prairie Provinces to 1953 with Biographical Index. 2nd. enl. ed., Toronto, University of Toronto Press, 1973.

438. Peirce, Charles Santiago Sanders. The Charles S. Peirce Papers. Cambridge, Mass., Harvard University Library Microreproduction Service, 1964. 32 reels.

    OTU mfm (L)   OWL   mfe (L)
    OTY mfm   OWTU mfm (LP)

    Guides: Robin, Richard S. Annotated Catalogue of the Papers of Charles S. Peirce, by Richard S. Robin. Amherst University of Massachusetts Press, 1967.

        Robin, Richard S. The Peirce Papers, a Supplementary Catalogue. Cambridge, Mass., Harvard University Library Microreproduction Service, 1970?

439. Peirce, Charles Santiago Sanders. Complete Works. Edited by Kenneth Laine Kerner. Greenwich, Conn., Johnson Associates, 1977.

    OGU mfe   OWTU mfe (L)

440. Penn, Thomas. The Thomas Penn Papers, 1729-1832, at the Historical Society of Pennsylvania. Philadelphia, Historical Society of Pennsylvania, 1968. 10 reels.

    QMG mfm (L)

441. Petites Revues D'Avant-Garde, Dadaistes, Surréalistes, ou Apparentées, 1912-1933. Paris, A.C.R.P.P.

   OOCC   mfm   (L)

   Guide: Petites Revues D'Avant-Garde, Dadaistes, Surréaliste, ou Apparentées. Index. Paris, A.C.R.P.P.

442. Phonefiche. Wooster, Ohio; Bell & Howell, 1977-

   OGU

   Guide: Community Cross-Reference Guide to Phonefiche: Current Telephone Directories on Microfiche. Wooster, Ohio, Bell & Howell, 1976-

443. Place, Francis. Papers of Francis Place (1771-1854) Illustrative of the Reform Crisis 1830-2. Wakefield, East Ardsley. Micro Methods Ltd.
   (Reproduced from original manuscripts, press cuttings, etc. in the departments of manuscripts and printed books of the British Museum).

   OTR   mfm   (11 reels.)   (L)

444. The Plains and the Rockies. Louisville, Lost Cause Press 1961-69? 537 vols.

   OGU   mcd

   Guide: The Plains and the Rockies: Lost Cause Press Microcard Collection. Louisville, Ky.: Lost Cause, 1969.

   Wagner, Henry R. The Plains and the Rockies; a Bibliography of Original Narratives of Travel and Adventure, 1800-1865; Rev. by C.L. Camp. 3d ed. Columbus, Long's College Book Co., 1953.

445. Porter, Peter Buel. Peter B. Porter Papers, (and those of his grandson, Peter A. Porter (1853-1925)) in the Buffalo and Erie County Historical Society. Buffalo, Buffalo and Erie County Historical Society, c1968. 13 reels.

   OSTCB   mfm   (LP)

   Guide: Guide to the Microfilm Edition of the Peter B. Porter Papers in the Buffalo and Erie County Historical Society. Lester W. Smith, Project Director, Arthur C. Detmers, Jr., Editor. Buffalo, Buffalo and Erie County Historical Society, 1968.

446. Praetorius, Michael. <u>Syntagma Musicum ex Veterum et Recentiorum, Ecclesiasticorum Autorum Lectione, 1615-1620</u>. Zug, Interdocumentation Co., Microfiche.

    OWA mfe (LP)

447. Prince Edward Island. Laws, Statutes, etc. <u>Statutes, 1867-1900</u>. Ottawa Candian Library Association. 3 reels.

    OGU mfm   OSUL mfm (LP)

448. Prince Edward Island. Legislative Assembly. <u>Journals, 1788-</u> Ottawa, Canadian Library Association. 11 reels.

    OGU mfm (1867-1900)   OPET mfm (1867-1900) (LP)

449. Prince Edward Island. Legislative Council. <u>Debates and Proceedings</u>. <u>1867-93</u>. Ottawa, Canadian Library Association.

    OGU mfm (1867-1893)   OPET mfm (1867-1893) (LP)

450. Prince Edward Island. Legislative Council. <u>Journals 1867-1893</u>, Ottawa, Canadian Library Association. 2 reels.

    OGU mfm

451. Prince Society. <u>Publications</u>. Boston. 1865-1920. 36 vols. Washington, D.C., Microcard Editions. 138 fiche.

    QLB mfe (L)

452. <u>Profile; Canadian Provincial and Municipal Publications, 1973-</u> Toronto, Micro Media Ltd. 1973-

    OGU   mfe   OPET mfe (selected items) (LP)
    OHM   mfe (LP)   OTY   mfe
    OKQ   mfe   OWA   mfe (LP)
    OLU   mfe (LP)   OWL   mfe (LP)
    OOCC mfe (P)   OWTU mfe (L)
    OOU   mfe (LP)   QMG   mfe (L)

    Guide: <u>Profile: Canadian and Municipal Publications</u>. 1973- Toronto, Micro Media Ltd., 1973- (issued annually with monthly updates)

453. Province in Rebellion: Documentary History of the Founding of the Commonwealth of Massachusetts, 1774-1775. Cambridge: Mass., Harvard University Press, 1975. 31 fiche and Book.

    OGU mfe   OTU mfe (LP)
    OKQ mfe (LP)   QMM mfe (LP)

454. Prussia. Landtag. Haus der Abgeordneten. Stenographische Berichte, 1849-1891. Washington, D.C., Microcard Editions, 1967.

    OLU mfe (1849-1870) (LP)   QMM mfe (1849-1891) (P)

455. Prussia. Landtag. Herrenhaus. Stenographische Berichte, 1849/50-1916/18. Washington, D.C., Microcard Edition, 1967-68.

    QMM mfe (1849-1891) (P)

456. Publicat; a Canadian Federal Documents Service, 1977- Toronto, Micromedia.

    OGU   mfe   OOU mfe (LP)
    OLU   mfe (LP)   OTY mfe
    OOCC mfe   OWL mfe (L)

    Guide: Publicat: A Canadian Federal Documents Service/un Service de Documents Federaux Canadiens. Toronto, Micromedia Ltd., 1977- (annual with monthly supplements)

457. Quebec. Commission Gendron. Documents de la Commission et Audiences Publiques. Quebec, Bibliothèque de la Legislature du Quebec, 1972.

    OOU mfm (LP)

458. Quebec. Ministère de l'Éducation. Office de la Langue Française. Centre de Terminologie. Fiches de Terminologie. Université Laval, Bibliotheque Centre de Documentation, 1972. 147 fiche.

    OSUL mfe (LP)

    Guide: Index du Fichies de Terminologie, 2 vols.

459. Quebec. (Province) Assemblée Nationale. Documents de la Session, 1867-1972. Quebec. Bibliothèque de la Session de la Province du Quebec.

    OOU mfm (1867-1972) (LP)   OTY mfm (1869-1973)

460. Quebec (Province) Législature. Assemblée Legislatif. <u>Journaux de la Chambre d'Assemblée Nationale du Bas-Canada, 1792-1837</u>. Quebec, Bibliotheque de la Législature du Quebec. 23 reels.

 OOU mfm (LP)   OTY mfm
 OPET mfm (LP)   QLB mfm (L)
 OSUL mfm (LP)

461. Quebec (Province) Législature. Conseil Législatif. <u>Journaux du Conseil Législatif de la Province du Bas-Canada, 1792-1837</u>. Montréal, Société Canadienne du Microfilm, 1974.

 OOU mfm (1802-1837) (LP) OTY mfm (1792-1837) (LP)
 OPET mfm (1792-1837) (LP) QLB mfm (1792-1837) (L)
 OSUL mfm (1792-1837) (LP)

462. Quebec (Province) Législature. Conseil Législatif. <u>Journaux du Conseil Législatif du Quebec 1867-1968</u>. Quebec, Bibliotheque de la Législature du Quebec. 1974.

 OOU mfm (LP)

463. Quebec (Province) Législature. Conseil Spécial. <u>Journaux du Conseil Spécial de la Province du Bas-Canada, 1838-1841</u>. Montréal. Société Canadienne du Microfilm, 1974.

 OOU mfm (1838-1841) (LP) OTY mfm (1838-1841)
 OPET mfm (1838-1840) (LP) QLB mfm (1838-1840) (L)

464. Radcliffe, Sir Joseph. <u>The Luddite Papers, 1812-1813</u>. Wakefield, Yorks, Micro Methods Ltd. (Reproduced from the original manuscripts in the archives at Rudding Park, Harrogate). 1 reel.

 OTR mfm (L)

465. <u>Radical Periodicals in the United States; 1890-1960</u>. New York: Greenwood Reprint Corp., 1968.

 OWTU mfm (L)

466. <u>Radical Periodicals of Great Britain, 1794-1950</u>. New York: Greenwood Reprint Corp., 1968. Microfiche.

 OWTU mfe (L)

467. Rare Militant British 19th Century Freethought Books. London: World Microfilm Publications, 1971. 14 reels and Index.

    OGU mfm

468. Die Recesse und Andere Akten der Hansetage von 1256-1430. Hrsg. Durch die Historische Commission Bei der Konigl. Academie der Wissenschaften. Leipzig, Duncker & Humblot, 1870-1897. Tumba, International Documentation Centre, 1964. 142 fiche.

    OTU mfm (LP)

469. Recessions, Depressions, and Economic Panics in American History: Collection of Sources, 1815-1974. Arlington, Va., University Publications of America, 1975. 7 reels with printed guide.

    OWL mfm (L)

470. Recueil des Historiens des Gaules et de la France, 1738-1904. 24 vols. Washington: Microcard Editions, 1966. 336 fiche.

    OGU mfe

471. Religion in America: Dissertations. Ann Arbor, University Microfilms, 1976. 47 reels.

    OHM mfm (LP)   OOU mfm (LP)

    Guide: Gaustad, E.S. Religion in America: an Annotated Bibliography of Selected Dissertations. Ann Arbor, Mich., University Microfilms 1976.

472. Religion in America: Early Books and Manuscripts. Ann Arbor, University Microfilms, 1976. 50 reels.

    OHM mfm (LP)   OOU mfm (LP)

    Guide: Gaustad, E.S. Religion in America: Early Books and Manuscripts: an Annotated Bibliography and Guide to the Microfilm Collection. Ann Arbor, Mich. University Microfilms International.

473. Rhoda Kellogg Child Art Collection. Washington, D.C., Microcard Editions, 1967. Microfiche. 255 fiche with index.

    OWA mfe (L)

474. Richardson, Samuel. <u>Correspondence, 1748-62.</u> Wakefield, Yorks, Micro Methods Ltd. 1969. (reproduced from the originals in the Victoria and Albert Museum, London)

   OTR mfm (L)

475. Rolle, Richard, of Hampole. <u>Prick of Conscience.</u> Wakefield, Yorks, Micro Methods Ltd. 1 reel.

   OTR mfm (L)

476. Roosevelt, Franklin D. <u>The Messages Between Franklin D. Roosevelt and Winston Churchill, 1939-1945, and Related Materials.</u> Washington, D.C., National Historical Publications Commission, Microfilm Publications Program, 1973. 6 reels.

   OHM mfm (LP)   QMM mfm (P)

477. Roosevelt, Franklin D. <u>The Press Conferences of Franklin D. Roosevelt, 1933-1945.</u> 2d ed. Washington, D.C., National Historical Publications Commission, Microfilm Publications Program, 1971. 13 reels.

   QLB mfm (L)

478. <u>Le Rousseauisme, 1788-1797.</u> Edited and Compiled by Roger Barny. Paris: Hachette Bibliotheque Nationale; New York: Clearwater Publishing, 1976. 87 fiche.
   (collection of works by contemporaries on Rousseau)

   OWTU mfe (L)

479. <u>Royal Alexandra Theatre, a Collection of Newspaper Clippings with Reviews of Stage Performances at This Theatre Toronto, 1911-65.</u> Toronto, University of Toronto Library Photocopy Services Unit, 1968. 7 reels.

   OTU mfm (LP)

480. Royal Institute for the Advancement of Learning. "Letter Books" 1820-1855. Letters, 1820-1849. Toronto, Canadian Microfilming.

   QMM mfm (P)

481. Russell Papers: Correspondence. v.p., 1863-1865. London, Public Record Office. 2 reels.

   OTU mfm (LP)

482. Russia. Gosudarstvennaia Duma. Gosudarstvennaĩa Duma. Extended-Micro Edition of International Documentation Centre AB. Tumba, Sweden Hagelby House. 132 fiche.

    OPAL mfe (L)

483. Russia. Laws, Statutes, etc. Polnoe Sobranie Zakonov Russiĭskoĭ Imperii 1649-1916. Sweden International Documentation Center.

    OOCC mfe   QMM mfe (P)

484. Russia. Treaties, etc. Recueil des Traites et Conventions Conclus par la Russie avec les Puissances Etrangeres. 15v. Washington, D.C., Microcard Editions. 147 fiche. (In Russian and French)

    OKQ mfe (LP)

485. Russia. Tsentral'nyĭ Statisticheskiĭ Komitet. Pervaĩa Vseobshchaĩa Perepis' Naseleniĩa Rossiskoĭ Imperii 1897g. New Haven, Conn., Research Publications.

    OOCC mfm (P)   OTU mfm (22 reels) (LP)

486. Russia. Tsentral'nyĭ Statisticheskiĭ Komitet. Statistika Rossiĭkoĭ Imperii, Petrograd, 1887-1916. Washington, D.C., Library of Congress Photoduplication. 8 reels.

    OLU mfm (LP)   OWTU mfm (some parts missing)

487. Russia. Voennoe Ministerstvo. Stoliẽtiẽ Voennago Ministerstva, 1802-1902. Zug. Switzerland, Interdocumentation, 1970?

    QMM mfe (P)

488. Russia (1917-   R.S.F.S.R.) Verkhovnyĭ Sovet. Vedomosti. Wooster, Ohio, Bell and Howell, 1961-   (in progress)

    OOCC mfm (P)

489. Russia (1923-   U.S.S.R.) S'ezd Sovetov. Stenograficheskiĭ Otchet, 1922-35. Washington, Hoover Institution Microfilms.

    OOCC mfm (P)

490. Russia (1923-   U.S.S.R.) Treaties, etc. <u>Sbornik Deĭstvuĭushchikh Dogorov, Soglashenii i Konventsii, 1928-1967</u>. Zug. Inter Documentation Co.

   OOCC   mfe   (P)

491. Russia (1923-   U.S.S.R.) Verkhovnyĭ Sovet. <u>Vedomosti</u>. Wooster, Ohio, Bell & Howell, 1961-   (In progress).

   OOCC   mfm   (P)

492. <u>Russia Letters</u>. s.l.n.d. London, Public Record Office, s.d. 10 reels.

   QSHERU   mfm   (L)

493. <u>Russian Futurism, 1910-1916 Poetry, Manifestoes, Journals and Miscellanies</u>. 54 Titles on Colour and Monochrome Microfiche. Cambridge: Chadwyck-Healey, 1977. (In Cyrillic). 77 fiche.

   OTU   mfm   (LP)

   Guide: Accompanied by Publisher's List of Titles and Introd. by the Editor (6 p.)

494. <u>Russian Historical Sources</u>. Series 1 and 2. New York, Readex Microprint, 1954-65.

   OHM   mpt   ser.1   (L)   OOU   mpt   ser.2   (LP)
   OKQ   mpt   ser.1-2   (L)   OSUL   mfe   ser.2   (L)
   OOCC mpt   ser.1-2   (L)   OTU   mpt   (LP)
                                    QMM   mpt   ser.1-2

495. <u>La Russie et l'Opinion Française au 19e Siècle</u>. Paris: Microeditions Hachette, 1972. (In French).

   OWTU mfe   (nos. 4-8, 10-11, 14-18, 24-29, 31-40, 43-44, 46-52, 66-67, 69-70, 72, 74-77, 79, 82)   (L)

496. Russkoe Istoricheskoe Obshchestvo, Leningrad. <u>Sbornik, 1-148; 1867-1916</u>. Ann Arbor, Michigan University Microfilms. 30 reels.

   QMM   mfm   (P)

497. <u>Sacrorum Conciliorum Nova et Amplissima Collectis</u> ... Washington, D.C., Microcard Editions, 1966.

   OLU   mfe   (LP)

498. Scadding, Henry. The Diaries of Henry Scadding; 1833-1837, 1844-1849, 1866-1889. Toronto, Microfilming Service. 2 reels. (Microfilm of manuscript in the Toronto Public Library made in 1958).

   OTU mfm (LP)

499. Scheibe, Johann Adolph. Johann Adolph Scheibens, Critischer Musikus. Neue Verm. Und Verb. Aufl. 1745. Zug, Inter Documentation. 13 fiche.

   OWA mfe (L)

500. Schein, Johann Hermann. Complete Collected Musical Works. 7v. 1901-1923. New York, University Music Editions, 1968. 29 fiche.

   OWA mfe (L)

501. Schomburg Center for Research in Black Culture. A Selection of Titles from the Schomberg Center for Research in Black Culture: Series 2. 1534-1955. 350v. Millwood, N.Y.: Distributed by Kraus-Thomson, 1965. 50 reels, and Index.

   OGU mfm

502. Scott, Sir Walter Bart. A Collection of Scarce and Valuable Tracts on the Most Entertaining Subjects, 1809-1815. 13 v. Louisville, Ky.: Lost Cause Press, 16 Microcards. (also known as Somers tracts)

   OGU mcd

503. Scottish Text Society, Edinburgh. Publications: no.1-65. 1884-1918. Washington: Microcard Editions, 1966. 230 fiche.

   OGU mfe   OTU mfe (LP)
   OLU mfe (LP)

504. Seventeenth Century English Pamphlets by Various Authors. From the Collection of the New York Public Library. New York, 1969. 1 reel.

   QMG mfm (L)

505. The Shaker Collection of Western Reserve Historical Society. Glen Rock, N.J., Microfilming Corporation of America, 1976. Microfilm. 123 reels.

   QMG mfm (L)

83.

506. Skeat, Walter William. Twelve Facsimilies of Old English Manuscripts; with Transcriptions and an Introduction by the Rev. Walter W. Skeat. Oxford, Clarendon Press, 1892. Wakefield, Yorks., Micro Methods.

    OTR (L)

507. The Slave Trade and Abolitionism in France and its Colonies, 1744-1848. 52v. Paris: Hachette, 1972-   228 fiche. (in French and with printed guide)

    OGU mfe

508. Slavery Source Materials. Washington, D.C., Microcard Editions, 1970. fiche.

    OLU mfe (LP)   OWTU mcd (L)

509. Smith, Goldwin. Goldwin Smith Papers at Cornell University, 1844-1915. Ithaca, N.Y., John M. Olin Library, 1971. 28 reels.

    OKQ mfm (LP)   OTU mfm (LP)

510. Social and Economic Development Plans. Zug, Switzerland, Inter-Documentation Company, 1968-   "Social and economic development plans from countries throughout the world"

    OKQ mfe (LP)   OOU mfe (Selected Countries)
    OLU mfe (LP)   (LP)
    OOCC mfe (Selected Countries)   OTU mfe

    Guide: Social and Economic Development Plans Microfiche Project. Zug, Switzerland, Inter-Documentation Company.

511. Social Problems and the Churches: the Harlan Paul Douglass Collection of Religious Research Reports. New Haven, Conn., Research Publications. 2731 fiche. With Printed Index.

    QMM mfe (P)

512. Société des Anciens Textes Français, Paris. Publications no.1-70, 1875-1925. Washington: Microcard Editions, 1965. 690 fiche.

    OGU mfe

513. Society for the Propagation of the Faith. Quebec (Diocese). <u>Rapport sur les Missions du Diocese de Quebec</u>. no.1-21, Jan 1839-Mai 1874. 21v. Louisville, Ky.: Lost Cause Press, 1960. 41 cards.

    OGU mcd

514. Society for the Propagation of the Gospel in Foreign Parts, London. East Ardsley, Eng., Micro Methods, Ltd., 1964.
(Received as part of British Records relating to America in Microform)
<u>Index to Letters, Ser. A.B. & C.</u>
<u>The Journals, with Appendices A-D v.1-50. 1701-1850</u> (London) 50v. in 54
<u>Letter Books. Ser. A, 1702-1737. Vols. 1-26.</u>
<u>Letters. Ser. B, 1701-1786.</u>
<u>Letters. Ser. C, vols. 1-15.</u>

    OTU mfm (LP)

515. <u>Somerset Parish Registers: Marriages, 1898-1915.</u> 15v. Washington, D.C., Microcard Editions.

    OGU mcd

516. Sotheby, Firm, Auctioneers, London. <u>Catalogue of Sales, 1734-1945.</u> Ann Arbor, Mich., University Microfilms, 1971-   381 reels.

    OTU mfm (LP)

517. <u>Source Materials in the Field of Theatre.</u> Ann Arbor, Mich., University Microfilms, 1967. 22 reels.

    OGU mfm   QQLA mfm (LP)
    OTU mfm (LP)

    Guide: Angotti, V.L. <u>Source Materials in the Field of Theatre an Annotated Bibliography and Subject Guide to the Microfilm Collection.</u> Ann Arbor, Mich., Xerox Education Division, University Microfilms Library Services 1967.

518. <u>South Africa; a Collection of Political Documents Covering the Years 1902-1963.</u> Stanford, Calif., Hoover Institution on War, Revolution, and Peace, 1967. 15 reels.

    OHM mfm (1912-1962) (LP)   OKQ mfm (LP)
                                                    OOCC mfm

519. Southey, Robert. <u>Poems in Letters to Walter London by Robert Southey Plus Additional Letters to W.S. Landor.</u> Wakefield, Yorks; Micro Methods Ltd. 1 reel.

    OTR mfm (L)

520. <u>Spanish Drama of the Golden Age.</u> New Haven, Conn., Research Publications, Inc. 86 reels.

    OHM mfm (LP)   OLU mfm (LP)

    Guide: Reguerro, Jose M. <u>Spanish Drama of the Golden Age; a Catalogue of the Comedia Collection in the University of Pennsylvania Libraries.</u> New York, Research Publications

521. <u>State Censuses, 1795-1934.</u> Millwood, New York, KTO Microform.

    OLU mfe (LP)

    Guide: Pubester, Henry J. <u>State Censuses: An Annotated Bibliography of Censuses of Population Taken After the Year 1790 by States and Territories of the United States.</u> New York, Burt Franklin, 1969 (reprint).

522. <u>State Succession Debates.</u> New Haven, Conn., Research Publications.

    OLU mfm (LP)

523. <u>Statistical Abstract of the United States, 1878-1955.</u> Washington, D.C., 1965. Microcard Editions, N.C.R. 500 fiche.

    OSUL mfe (L)

524. Statistics Canada. <u>Publications, 1841-1975.</u> Toronto, Micromedia Ltd., 1976.

    OOU mfe (LP)

525. Stevens, Benjamin Franklin, comp. <u>Facsimiles of Manuscripts in European Archives Relating to America, 1773-1783.</u> v.1-25. New York, Ams Press Film Service, 1971? 14 reels.

    OWA mfe (L)

526. Strachan, John. <u>Papers.</u> Toronto Ontario Dept. of Public Records and Archives, 1959. 13 reels.

    OHM mfm (LP)

527. The Stuart Papers from the Denys Eyre Bower Collection, Chiddingstone Castle, Kent. East Ardsley, Wakefield, Yorks., Micro Methods, 1969. 3 reels.
"Manuscripts and letters from the 16th to 19th centuries by and about Stuart family".

OHM mfm (LP)

528. The Stuart Papers from the Royal Archives in Windsor Castle, Windsor Castle, Royal Archives. East Ardsley, Yorks., Micro Methods. 246 reels.

OHM mfm (P)

529. Tanjur. Cone Tanjur. 209v. Washington, D.C., Library of Congress, Photo Duplication Service, 1974? (text in Tibetan).

OTU mfe (LP)

530. Teapot Dome Documents. Edited by John Mascato. Arlington, Va., University Publications of America, 1975. 7 reels with Printed Guide.

OWL mfm (L)

531. Le Théatre de la Révolution et de l'Empire: 132 Pièces de Théatre/ Selectionnées et Présentées par Marc Regaldo; avec le Concours du Centre d'Etudes du XVIIIe Siècle, Université de Bordeaux. --- Paris: Microeditions Hachette: Distributed by Clearwater Pub. Co., 1975. 167 fiche.

QMM mfe (P)

532. Theiner, Augustin. Monuments Historiques Relatifs aux Règnes d'Alexis Michaelowitch, Feodor III, et Pierre le Grand, Czars de Russie, Extraits des Archives du Vatican et de Naples. Zug, Switzerland, Inter-Documentation Co. 19 fiche.

QMM mfe (P)

533. Thomason Tracts. Ann Arbor, Mich., Xerox University Microfilms, 1977-

OHM mfm (LP)   OTU mfm (LP)
OKQ mfm (LP)

533.   (Cont'd)

Guide: British Museum. Dept. of Printed Books. Thomason Collection. <u>Catalogue of Pamphlets Books, Newspapers, and Manuscripts Relating the Civil War, the Commonwealth and Restoration, Collected by George Thomason 1640-1661</u>. London, Printed by Order to the Trustees, 1908.

University Microfilms, Ann Arbor, Mich. <u>Early English Books 1641-1700; a Partial List of Microfilms by Wing Numbers, 7th Year</u>. University Microfilms, Ann Arbor, Mich., 1967.

534. Three Centuries of Drama. (English Drama, 1500-1800 and American Drama, 1741-1830). Compiled by Henry W. Wells. New York, Readex Microprint, 1955-56.

OGU	mpt		OTU	mpt	(L)
OHM	mpt	(L)	OTY	mpt	
OKQ	mpt	(L)	OWA	mpt	(L)
OLU	mpt	(LP)	QMM	mpt	
OOCC	mpt				

Guide: Bergquist, G. William, ed. <u>Three Centuries of English and American Plays, a Checklist. England: 1500-1800; United States: 1714-1830</u>. New York, Hafner, 1963.

535. Three Centuries of French Drama. v.p. 1600-1899. Washington, D.C., Microcard Editions; Lexington, Falls City Press, 1957-

OTU   mcd   (LP)   OWA   mcd   (L)

Guide: Thompson, L.S. <u>A Bibliography of French Plays on Microcards</u>. Hamden, Conn., Shoe String Press, 1967.

536. The Timothy Pickering Papers. Frederick S. Allis, Jr., Editor. Boston, Massachusetts Historical Society 1966. (Microfilm Publication Number 2)

OLU   mfm   (LP)

Guide: <u>Guide to the Microfilm Edition of the Timothy Pickering Papers</u>. Boston, Massachusetts Historical Society, 1966.

537. Toronto Stock Exchange. <u>Company Reports</u>. Middletown, Conn., Godfrey Memorial Library, 1960-   "Annual reports of companies listed on the Toronto Stock Exchange."

OTU   mcd   (1961-1965)   (LP)   QMG   mfe   (L)

538. Trades Union Congress. Parliamentary Committee. <u>Minutes, 1888-1922.</u>
London, World Microfilm Publications, 1974. 5 reels.

    QMM mfm (P)

539. <u>TRANSDEX; JPRS</u> Documents. no.63/63849-70370/70401-   Wooster, Ohio,
Bell & Howell Micro Photo Division 1975-   (formerly issued in
separate series, e.g. East Europe, international developments,
China and Asian developments, etc.)

    OTU mfm (JPRS nos. 63778-70401) 112 reels
            mfe (70402-)
    OWTU mfe
    QMM mfe (P)

    Guide: <u>Indexed in the Monthly Catalog of United States Government
Publications.</u> Reels for 1977 Accompanied by Monthly Printed
Indices with Title: **TRANSDEX** Index Which are Superseded by
Annual Comulation Published in Microform.

540. <u>Travels in the New South, 1865-1955.</u> Louisville, Lost Cause Press.
(in progress)

    OGU mcd

    Guide: Clark, Thomas D. <u>Travels in the New South; a Bibliography.</u>
Norman, Univ. of Oklahoma Press, 1962.

541. <u>Travels in the Old South, 1527-1860.</u> Louisville, Lost Cause Press.
(in progress)

    OGU mcd

    Guide: Clark, Thomas D. <u>Travels in the Old South; a Bibliography.</u>
Norman, Univ. of Oklahoma Press, 1956-59.

542. <u>Tson-Kha-Pa Blo-Bzan-Grags-Pa, 1357-1419.</u> Yab Sras Gsun Bum/Tson Kha
Pa (Rje) Stoney Brook, N.Y. Institute for Advanced Studies of
World Religions 1976. 266 fiche. (In Tibetan)

    OTU mfe (LP)

543. <u>Tudor Facsimile Texts</u> (under the supervision and editorship of John S.
Farmer) New York, AMS Press, 1907-1914. New York, AMS Press
Film Service. 4 reels.

    OWA mfm (LP)

543.   (Cont'd)

    Guide: The Tudor Facsimile Texts; Old English Plays: Printed and Manuscript Rarities, Edited by John S. Farmer. New York, AMS Press.

544.   Turkey Letters. s.l.n.d. (London, Public Record Office, s.d.) 18 reels.

    QSHERU   mfm   (L)

545.   Underground and Alternative Press in Britain. Brighton, Eng.: Harvester Press, 1974.

    OWTU   mfe   covers 1965-1975   (LP)   mfm   covers 1965-1973   (LP)

    Guide: The Underground and Alternative Press in Britain: a Bibliographical Guide. Hassocks, Eng., Harvester Press. 1974-

546.   United Nations. A Doctoral Dissertation Collection, 1866-   Ann Arbor, University Microfilms International, 1977-

    OGU   mfm   (reels 1-   )

547.   United Nations Documents and Official Records, 1946-   New York, Readex Microprint Corp., 1952-

OHM	mpt	(LP)	OSUL	mpt	(1964-1969)	(L)
OKQ	mpt	(L)	OTU	mpt	1946-	
OLU	mpt	(LP)	OTY	mpt	1946-	
OOCC	mpt		OWA	mpt	1969-	(L)
OOU	mpt	(L)	OWL	mpt	1946-	(L)
OPET	mpt	(L)	QMG	mpt	1946-	(L)

    Guides: Brimmer, Brenda et al. A Guide to the use of United Nations Documents (Including Reference to the Specialized Agencies and Special U.N. Bodies) Dobbs Ferry, N.Y.: Oceana, 1962.

    United Nations. Dag Hammerskjold Library. Index to Proceedings of General Assembly. New York: United Nations, 5th- , 1950/51-

    United Nations. Dag Hammerskjold Library. United Nations Documents Index: Cumulative Checklist. New York: United Nations, v.14- , 1963-   .

    United Nations. Dag Hammerskjold Library. United Nations Documents Index: Cumulative Index. New York: United Nations, v.14- , 1963-   .

547. (Cont'd)

United Nations. Dag Hammerskjold Library. <u>United Nations Documents Index</u>. New York: United Nations, v.1- . Jan. 1950-

United Nations, Dept. of Public Information. <u>Ten Years of United Nations Publications, 1945-1955, a Complete Catalogue</u>. New York, 1955.

548. United Society for the Propagation of the Gospel. African Archives of the USPG London. <u>MSS Records for Natal (Maritzburg) c1853-1900</u>. East Ardsley, Wakefield, Yorks. Micro Methods, 1971. 13 reels.

QMM   mfm   (P)

549. U.S. Bureau of Indian Affairs. Commissioner. <u>Annual Reports 1824-1949</u>. Washington, D.C., Microcard Editions. 554 cards.

OOCC   mcd   OWTU   mfe
OPET   mcd

550. U.S. Bureau of the Census. <u>Census Publications 1790-1916</u>. Washington, National Archives of the United States.

OLU   mfm   (LP)

Guides: Dubester, Henry J. <u>Catalogue of the United States Census Publications 1790-1945</u>. Washington, Government Printing Office, 1950.

United States. Superintendent of Documents. <u>Monthly Catalogue of United States Government Publications</u>. Washington, D.C., Government Printing Office.

551. U.S. Bureau of the Census. <u>Decennial Census Publications, 1900-1960</u>. Westport, Greenwood Pr., 1973.

QMM   mfm   (P)

552. U.S. Bureau of the Census. <u>Federal Population Censuses, 1790-1890</u>. Washington, National Archives, 1967. 183 reels.

OKQ   mfm   (LP)

Guides: <u>U.S. National Archives. Federal Population Censuses, 1790-1890</u>. Washington, 1966.

<u>Index to American Federal Censuses, 1790-1890</u>. Prepared by the Documents Units, Douglas Library, Queen's University, 1971.

553.   U.S. Bureau of the Census. Seventeenth Decennial Census, 1950.
       Westport, Conn., Greenwood Press.

       OLU   mfm   (LP)

       Guide: United States. Superintendent of Documents. Monthly Cata-
               logue of United States Government Publications. Washington,
               D.C., Government Printing Office.

554.   U.S. Bureau of the Census. Sixteenth Decennial Census 1940.
       Westport, Conn., Greenwood Press.

       OLU   mfm   (LP)

       Guides: United States. Superintendent of Documents. Monthly Cata-
               logue of United States Government Publications. Washington,
               D.C., Government Printing Office.

               Dubester, Henry J. Catalogue of United States Census
               Publications 1790-1945. Washington, Government Printing
               Office, 1950.

555.   U.S. Bureau of the Census. Statistical Abstracts of the United States.
       1878-1955. Washington, D.C., Microcard Editions, 500 fiche.

       OOCC mcd   OSUL mfe   (L)
       OPET mcd   (LP)

556.   U.S. Commissioner of Indian Affairs. Annual Report, 1824-1949.
       Washington, D.C. Microcard Editions.

       OOCC mcd   (P)   OWTU mfe
       OPET mcd   (1850-1949)

557.   U.S. Congress. American State Papers, 1789-1838. Serial Set,
       15th Congress 1817-
       "This collection contains both the journals of the House of Congress
       and the scores of documents submitted to that body".

       OGU   mpt   (1833-1861)   OLU   mpt   (LP)
       OHM   mpt   (LP)   OSTCB mfe   (L)
       OKQ   mpt   (L)   OTY   mpt   (1776-1838)

       Serial Set
       OHM   mpt   ser. nos.1307-2160, 1867-83   (L)
       OLU   mpt   (1817-1901) (LP)
       OTY   mpt   ser. nos.1-2676, 1817-1889

558. U.S. Congress. <u>Committee Hearings, Prints, 81st.-84th. Congress, 1949-56</u>. Ann Arbor, University Microfilms, 1950-1957. New York, Readex Microprint Corp.

    OHM   mpt (L)   QMG   mfe (L)
    OTU   mfm/mpt

559. U.S. Congress. <u>Committee Hearings, Prints, 85th-87th</u> (2nd session) <u>Congress, 1957-1962</u>. New York, Readex Microprint Corp., 1957-1963.

    OHM   mpt (L)   OTU   mfm/mpt
    OKQ   mpt (85th-90th, 1957-1969)   QMG   mfe (L)

    Guide: U.S. Superintendent of Documents. <u>Monthly Catalog of U.S. Government Publications</u>. Washington, Gov't Print. Off., 1895 to Date. (not all Committee prints are indexed in the monthly catalog)

560. U.S. Congress. <u>Congressional Globe. Twenty-Third Congress, Dec. 2 1833-Forty-Second Congress, March 3, 1873</u>. Washington, Gales and Seaton, 1834-73.

    OHM   mcd (L)   OTY   mfe
    OLU   mfe (L)   OWA   mfe (L)
    OOCC mcd (P)   OWTU mfe
    OTU   mfm

561. U.S. Congress. <u>Congressional Record, Forty-Third Congress, Dec. 1, 1873-</u> Washington, U.S. Gov't Print. Off., 1969.

    OSUL mfm (1962-1968, 1971-72) (LP)   OWA   mfm 1873-1968 (LP)
    OTU   mfm   OWTU mfm 1873-
    OTY   mfm   QMM   mfm 1873-

562. U.S. Congress. <u>The Debates and Proceedings in the Congress of the U.S., First Session, March 3, 1789- Eighteenth Session, May 27, 1824</u>. Washington, Gales and Seaton, 1834-56.

    OOCC   mcd (P)   OTU   mfm
    OSTCB mfm (L)

563. U.S. Congress. <u>Register of Debates in the Congress of the U.S. Second Session of the Eighteenth Congress, Dec. 6, 1824- First Session of the Twenty-Fifth Congress, Oct. 16, 1837</u>. Washington, Gales and Seaton, 1825-37.

    OHM   mfm (LP)   OTU   mfm   OWA   mfm
    OOCC mcd (P)   OTY   mfm (L)   OWTU mfm (6 reels)

564.   U.S. Consulate General. Hongkong. Selections from China Mainland
       Magazines. no.1-   Aug. 15, 1955- Hong Kong. Washington, Library
       of Congress Photoduplication Service. 19 reels. "Translations of
       articles appearing in Chinese Communist periodicals".

       OTU   mfm   (LP)

565.   U.S. Consulate General. Hong Kong. Survey of China Mainland Press.
       Nov.1, 1950-   Dec. 1957. Hong Kong. Washington, Library of
       Congress Photoduplication Service. 36 reels. "Translations of
       articles appearing in Chinese Communist newspapers or releases
       emanating from Chinese Communist news agencies".

       OTU   mfm   (LP)

566.   U.S. Consulate General. Hong Kong. Agricultural Attache's Office.
       Agricultural Information on Mainland China, 1953-1967/ U.S. Hong
       Kong Agricultural Attache. Washington, D.C., Center for Chinese
       Research Materials, Association of Research Libraries, 1970.
       5 reels.

       OTU   mfm   (LP)

567.   U.S. Consulate General. Hong Kong. Agricultural Attache's Office.
       Collection of Agricultural Information on Mainland China, 1948-1967.
       Washington, D.C., Cooper-Trent Division, Keuffel and Esser, 1967.
       55 reels.

       OTU   mfm   (LP)

       Guide: Accompanied by a 'General Table of Contents Parts 1 & II'
              (ii, 29 leaves) Supplied by the Publisher.

568.   U.S. Dept. of State. Consular Despatches, 1790-1906. Washington,
       National Archives and Records Service.

       OLU   mpt   (1790-1906)   (LP)   OTU   mfm   (1790-1906) (LP)
       OOU   mfm   (1790-1906)   (LP)   QMG   mfm   (selected items) (L

       Guide: U.S. National Archives. List of National Archives Microfilm
              Publications, 1968. Washington National Archives and Record
              Service, 1968.

569.   U.S. Dept. of State. Despatches from United States Consuls, Hamilton,
       Ont. 1867-1906. Washington, D.C., National Archives and Records
       Service.

       OHM   mfm   (LP)

570. U.S. Dept. of State. <u>Despatches from United States Ministers to China, 1843-1906.</u> Washington, D.C., U.S. National Archives Microfilm Publications. (Publication M 92) 131 reels.

    QMM mfm (P)

571. U.S. Dept. of State. <u>Despatches from United States Ministers to Great Britain, 1791-1906.</u> Washington, National Archives and Record Service, 1954. 200 reels.

OKQ	mfm	(v.13-18)	(LP)	OTU	mfm	(July 1819-1906)	(LP)
OLU	mfm	(LP)		QMG	mfm	(selected items)	(L)
OOU	mfm	(LP)					

572. U.S. Dept. of State. <u>Diplomatic Instructions of the Department of State, 1801-1906.</u> Washington, National Archives, 1945-46.

    OTU mfm (LP)

573. U.S. Dept. of State. Foreign Relations of the United States. <u>Diplomatic Papers, 1861-1956.</u> 209v. Washington, D.C., Microcard Editions.

OKQ	mfm	(1861-1946)	(L)	OSUL	mfe	(L)	
OLU	mfm	(1861-1956)	(LP)	OTU	mfm	(P)	
OOCC	mcd	(1861-1942)	(L)	OWA	mfe	(1861-1942)	(LP)
OPET	mcd	(1886-1920)	(L)	QMG	mfe	(1861-1920)	(L)
OSTCB		(1913-45)	(P)	QMM	mfe	(1867-1945)	
				QQLA	mfe	(L)	
				QSHERU	mfe	(L)	

Guide: Reel Indexes: 1861-1899 see reel 19
                           1900-1918 see reel 30
                           1919-1956 list printed at beginning of each year

574. U.S. Dept. of State. <u>Miscellaneous Letters of the Dept. of State, 1789-1906.</u> Washington, National Archives, 1949. 12 reels.

    OKQ mfm (Jan. 3, 1806-Dec. 29, 1815) (LP)

575. U.S. Dept. of State. <u>Notes from the British Legation in the United States to the Department of State, 1791-1906.</u> Washington, D.C., National Archives, 1943.

    OLU mfm (1791-1906) (LP)   OTU mfm (1791-1825) (LP)

576. U.S. Dept. of State. <u>Notes from the Department of State to Foreign Ministers and Consuls in the U.S. 1793-1834</u>. Washington, National Archives, 1943.

   OTU   mfm   (LP)

577. U.S. Dept. of State. <u>Notes to Foreign Legations in United States from the Department of State. Great Britain, 1834-1906</u>. Washington, National Archives, 1949.

   OTU   mfm   (LP)

578. U.S. Department of State. <u>Papers Relating to the Foreign Relations of the United States, 1861-1942</u>. Washington, D.C. Microcard Editions, Inc. 1966.

   OSUL   mfe   (L)

579. U.S. Dept. of State. <u>Records of Negotiations Connected with the Treaty of Ghent; Despatches from the American Commissioners, Aug. 29, 1813-July 3, 1815</u>. Washington, National Archives, 1942. 2 reels.

   OKQ   mfm   (LP)

580. U.S. Dept. of State. <u>Records of the U.S. Consulate in Kumming, 1922-28</u>. Washington, D.C., National Archives and Records Service, 1959.

   QMM   mfm   (P)

581. U.S. Dept. of State. <u>The Revolutionary Diplomatic Correspondence of the U.S. 1889</u>. Washington, Microcard Editions.

   OSTCB   mfe   (L)

582. U.S. Dept. of the Army. Caribbean Defense Command. <u>Panama Canal Studies</u>. Washington, Library of Congress, 1976.

   OLU   mfm   (LP)

583. U.S. Dept. of the Treasury. <u>Annual Reports of the Secretary of the Treasury on the State of Finances 1790-1974</u>. Washington, D.C., University Publications of America, Inc. (with printed guides) 31 reels.

   OWTU   mfm

584. U.S. Educational Resources Information Center. (Papers from ca. 18 Clearinghouses on): <u>1. Adult Education; 2. Disadvantaged; 3. Educational Technology; 4. Rural Education; 5. Reading; 6. Library and Information Science; etc.</u> Bethesda, Md., 1970- (in progress)

    OGU   mfe   1-6   QMG   mfe   (L)
    OKQ   mfe   1-4 (L)   QMM   mfe   (complete to date)
    OLU   mfe   (LP)   (P)
    OOU   mfe   (LP)   QQLA   mfe   (L)
                                          QRUQR mfe   (no. 1)

    Guide: U.S. Educational Resources Information Center. <u>Catalog of Selected Documents on the Disadvantaged.</u> (ERIC Educational Documents Index, 1966-1969) New York: CCM Information Corp., 1970.

585. U.S. Educational Resources Information Center. <u>ERIC Documents.</u> Washington, D.C., Microcard Editions, 1966-

    OOCC   mfe   1970-   (selected items)
    OPET   mfe   (L)
    OWA   mfe   1956-73 (L)
    QMM   mfe   1973-

    Guide: U.S. Educational Resources Information Center. <u>How to Use ERIC.</u> Washington: U.S. Dept. of Health, Education and Welfare, Office of Education, 1971.

586. U.S. Embassy. France. <u>The U.S. and France: Correspondence Dealing with Economic Relations, 1811-1930.</u> Wilmington, Del., Library of Congress for Scholarly Resources, Inc. (n.d.) 7 reels.

    OKQ   mfm

587. U.S. Federal Bureau of Investigation. <u>Uniform Crime Reports, 1930-72.</u> Englewood, Conn., Microcard Editions.

    OOCC   mfe   (P)

588. U.S. Foreign Broadcast Information Service. <u>Daily Report.</u> Washington, Library of Congress Photoduplication 1972.

    OTU   mfm   (Aug. 4, 1970-Dec. 10, 1971. Covering Communist China, Eastern Europe, Soviet Union) (P)

589. U.S. Joint Publications Research Service. <u>JPRS Publications.</u> Annapolis, Md., Research and Microfilms, 1961-68; New York, CCM Information Corp., 1969- N.B. Microprint Edition Included in U.S. Government Publications, ser. 2, q.v.

589.   (Cont'd)

   OTU mfm (P)   OWTU mfm

   Translations and Abstracts Issued in Several Subseries, the Most Important of Which are:

   1. China and Asia (formerly 2 series: China, (and) Asian Developments). (in progress)

      OTU   mfm (P)   QMM mfm (1962-1970) (P)
      OWTU mfm (1972-197 -   )

   2. East Europe; Selected Economic Translations.

      OKQ mfm v.8-   (L)   OWTU mfm (reels 236-244)
      OTU mfm   (P)

   3. International Developments (translations in the social sciences emanating from Africa, Latin America, Near East and Western Europe).

      OTU mfm (P)   OWTU mfm (reels 233-245) (P)

   4. Scholarly Book Translation Series. 1957-63, 32 reels.

      OHM mfm (577/D-23856) (LP)   OTU mfm (P)

   5. Indonesia. 1957-61. 5 reels.

      OKQ mfm (L)   QMM mfm (P)

   6. Soviet Union (translations in the social sciences emanating from the USSR)

      OTU mfm (P)   OWTU mfm (1969-1974)

   7. Mongolia, 1957-61. 2 reels.

      OKQ mfm (L)   OTU mfm (P)

   8. North Korea, 1957-61. 8 reels.

      OKQ mfm (L)   QMM mfm (P)
      OTU mfm (P)

589. (Cont'd)

  Guides: Catalogue Cards in Book Form for United States Joint Publications Research Service Translations. Annapolis, Md., Research and Microfilm Publications, 1959-1968. New York, CCM Information Corp., 1969-1970.

  China and Asia (exclusive of Near East), Bibliography-Index to U.S. JPRS Research Translations. Annapolis, Research and Microfilm Publications, v.3, no.3 v.8, July 1964, June 1965-1970.

  East Europe; Bibliography-Index to U.S. JPRS Research Translations. Annapolis, Research and Microfilm Publications, 1962-1970.

  International Developments. A Bibliography. Annapolis, Research and Microfilm Publications, v.1, July/Sept. 1962-1970.

  Soviet Union; Bibliography - Index to U.S. JPRS Research Translations. Annapolis, Research and Microfilm Publications, v.1-8, July/Sept. 1962-1970.

  Subject Index to the U.S. Joint Publications Research Service Translations. Annapolis, Research and Microfilm Publications Jan./June 1966-1968.

  Transdex: Bibliography and Index to the United States Joint Publications Research Service (JPRS) Translations. New York, CCM Information Corp., v.9, 1971-

590. U.S. Joint Publications Research Service. Weekly Report on Communist China Prepared by Foreign Documents Division, Central Intelligence Agency. Washington, D.C., 1959-1960.

  QMM   mfm   1959-60   (P)

591. U.S. Library of Congress. Cyrillic Union Catalogue. New York, Readex Microprint Corp., 1963. (with index)

  OTU   mpt

592. U.S. Library of Congress. Manuscript Division. Presidential Papers. U.S. Library of Congress, 1958-

  OTU   mfm   (selected Presidents: Chester A. Arthur, William Henry Harrison, Andrew Jackson, James Monroe, Franklin Pierce, Zachary Taylor, John Tyler and Martin Van Buren) (LP)

592.   (Cont'd)

        Guides: U.S. Library of Congress. Manuscript Division. <u>Index to the Chester A. Arthur Papers</u>. U.S. Government Printing Office, 1961.

        U.S. Library of Congress. Manuscript Division. <u>Index to the William Henry Harrison Papers</u>. U.S. Government Printing Office, 1960.

        U.S. Library of Congress. Manuscript Division. <u>Index to the Andrew Jackson Papers</u>. U.S. Government Printing Office, 1967.

        U.S. Library of Congress. Manuscript Division. <u>Index to the James Monroe Papers</u>. U.S. Government Printing Office, 1963.

        U.S. Library of Congress. Manuscript Division. <u>Index to the Franklin Pierce Papers</u>. U.S. Government Printing Office, 1962.

        U.S. Library of Congress. Manuscript Division. <u>Index to the Zachary Taylor Papers</u>. U.S. Government Printing Office, 1960.

        U.S. Library of Congress. Manuscript Division. Index to the John Tyler Papers. U.S. Government Printing Office, 1961.

593. U.S. National Archives. <u>Collection of Hungarian Political and Military Records, 1909-1945</u>. Washington, U.S., National Archives Microfilm Publications, 1972.

    OTU mfm (LP)

    Guide: United States. National Archives. <u>Guide to the Collection of Hungarian Political and Military Records, 1909-45</u>, Washington, 1972.

594. U.S. National Archives. <u>Records of the Russian-American Company, 1802-1867</u>. Washington, National Archives, 1934. 77 reels.

    OKQ mfm (LP)

595. U.S. Navy Dept. <u>Letters Received by the Secretary of the Navy: Captain's Letters, 1805-1886</u>. Washington, National Archives, 1947.

    OKQ mfm (Jan. 1, 1812-Dec. 29, 1815) (LP)

596. U.S. Navy Dept. Letters Received by Secretary of the Navy from Commanders, 1804-1886. Washington, National Archives, 1954. 3 reels.

   OKQ mfm (Jan. 1, 1810-Dec. 30, 1816) (LP)

597. U.S. Navy Dept. Letters Received by the Secretary of the Navy from Officers Below the Rank of Commander, 1802-1884. Washington, National Archives, 1959. 5 reels.

   OKQ mfm (June 30th, 1815-June 2, 1881) (LP)

598. U.S. Navy Dept. Letters Sent by the Secretary of the Navy to Officers, 1798-1868. Washington, National Archives, 1950. 3 reels.

   OKQ mfm (v.1-12, Mar. 28, 1812-Apr. 30, 1817) (LP)

599. U.S. Navy Dept. Records of the United States Exploring Expedition Under the Command of Lieutenant Charles Wilkes, 1838-1842. Washington, National Archives, 1944. 27 reels.

   OKQ mfm (LP)

   Guide: Bibliographical Notes on reel 1. Index to the Records of the United States Exploring Expedition Under the Command of Lieutenant Charles Wilkes, 1838-1842. Washington, National Archives.

600. U.S. Office of Strategic Services. Intelligence and Research Reports. Washington, University Publications of America, Inc., 1976. (with index)

   OWTU mfm (pt.2, Postwar Japan, Korea and southeast Asia, pt.3, China and India pt.4, Germany and its occupied territories during World War II. Pt. 5, Postwar Europe. Pt.6, The Soviet Union. Pt.7, The Middle East) (P)

   QMM mfm (Pts.2, 3, 7) (P)

601. U.S. President's Commission on the Assassination of President Kennedy. Hearings and Reports, 1964. Princeton, N.J., Princeton Microfilm Corp. 1967. 7 reels.

   OWA mfm (LP)

602. U.S. President's Commission on the Assassination of President Kennedy. (Warren Commission). <u>Hearings</u>. Glen Rock, New Jersey, Microfilming Corporation of America.

    OLU mfm (LP)

603. U.S. Secretary of State. <u>Press Conferences, 1922-1973</u>. Wilmington, Scholarly Resources, Inc., 1974.

    OWTU mfe

604. U.S. Superintendent of Documents. <u>Government Publications</u>. ser.1, 1956- (Depository) ser.2, 1953- (Non depository) New York, Readex Microprint Corp.

OKQ	mpt	ser.1, 1968-	ser.2, 1958-	(L)
OLU	mpt	ser.1, 1970-	ser.2, 1970-	(LP)
OTU	mpt	ser.1, 1956-	ser.2, 1962-	
OTY	mpt	ser.1, 1956-	ser.2, 1955-	
QMG	mpt	ser.1, 1958-	(L)	

    Guide: United States. Superintendent of Documents. <u>Monthly Catalogue of United States Government Publications</u>. Washington, D.C., Government Printing Office, 1895-

605. U.S. War Dept. <u>Letters Received by the Secretary of War: Registered Series, 1801-1806</u>. Washington, D.C., National Archives, 1954. 30 reels.

    OKQ mfm (Sept. 1811-Dec. 1812, A-Z; July 1812-May 1814, A-Z; May 1814-Dec. 1815, A-Z; June 1815 - Dec. 1816, A-R) (LP)

606. U.S. War Dept. <u>Letters Received by the Secretary of War: Unregistered Series, 1789-1860</u>. Washington, D.C., National Archives, 1954. 14 reels.

    OKQ mfm (1812, A-W; 1813, A-W; 1814, A-Z; 1815, A-W) (LP)

607. U.S. War Dept. <u>Letters Sent by the Secretary of War, Relating to Military Affairs, 1800-1861</u>. Washington, D.C., National Archives, 1963. 6 reels.

    OKQ mfm (v.3-8, May 1, 1806 - Dec. 30, 1814) (LP)

608. U.S. War Dept. Records of the Secretary of War, Letters Sent to the President, 1800-1863. Washington, D.C., National Archives, 1948. 1 reel.

    OKQ mfm (v.1, Nov. 13, 1800 - Jan. 6, 1820, index, 1800-1840) (LP)

609. University of Oregon. School of Health, Physical Education and Recreation. Microform Publications (Doctoral dissertations, masters theses and scholarly out-of-print books)

    OGU mfe   OOU mcd/mfe (LP)
    OLU mcd/mfe (LP)

    Guide: Health, Physical Education and Recreation Microforms Publication Bulletin. Eugene, Oregon, University of Oregon School of Health, Physical Education and Recreation.

610. Upcott Collection of Literary Autographs, 1765-1830. (with printed index) Bishop's Stortford, Eng., Chadwyck-Healey. 1975. 6 reels.

    OHM mfm (LP)

611. Upper Canada (1791-1840). The Upper Canada Gazette or American Oracle, April 18, 1793-   May 1, 1845. Ottawa, Canadian Library Association.

    OPET mfm (1793-1845) (LP)   QMM mfm (1793-1845) (P)

612. Urban Canada/Canada Urbain; Toronto, Micromedia Ltd., 1977-

    OGU mfe   OOU mfe (LP)
    OHM mfe (LP)   OTU mfe (LP)
    OKQ mfe (L)   OWL mfe (L)
    OOCC mfe (P)

    Guide: Urban Canada, a Current Index to Canadian Publications in the Field of Urban and Regional Planning and Development. 1977- . Toronto, Micromedia Ltd. (in progress)

613. Urban Documents Microfiche Collection. (as cited and indexed in 'index to current Urban documents'). Local Government Documents from the Wood Press, Microform Dept.

    OWTU mfe (L)

614. Utopias au Siècle des Lumières. Paris, Microeditions Hachette, 197-
    (In French)

    OKQ mfe (LP)

615. Van Marum, Martinus. Van Marum Collection: Manuscripts of Essays, Lecture Notes, Diaries. East Ardsley: EP. Microform, 1976?-
    349 fiche. (Manuscripts preserved in the Hollandsche Maatschappij der Wetenschappen, Haarlem). With index.

    OTU mfe (LP)

616. Vassall, William. Letter Books, 1769-1800. Introduction by Walter Minchinton. East Ardsley, Eng., Micro Methods Ltd., 1963. (Received as part of British records relating to America in microform).

    OTU mfm (LP)

    Guide: Crick, B.R. and Mariam Alman, eds. A Guide to Manuscripts Relating to America in Great Britain and Ireland. Oxford University for the British Association for American Studies, 1961.

617. Vatikanische Quellen zur Geschichte der Papstlichen Hof-und Finanzverwaltung, 1316-1378. Zug, Switzerland, Interdocumentation Co., 19- . 50 fiche.

    OKQ mfe (LP)

618. Vega Carpio, Lope Felix de. Comedias. Barcelona, S. de Cormellas, London, British Museum Photographic Service, 1966. 5 reels.

    OTU mfm (LP)

619. Vega Carpio, Lope Felix de. Copy and Holograph MSS. Wakefield, England, Micro Methods, 1971. 5 reels.

    OKQ mfm (LP)

620. Vega Carpio, Lope Felix de. Printed Plays of Lope de Vega and Others. Wakefield, England, Micro Methods, 1971. 2 reels.

    OKQ mfm (LP)

621. Verreau. Hospice Anthelme. <u>Fonds Verreau: du Carton I au Carton IX</u>. Quebec. Seminaire de Quebec, s.d. Quebec, Univ. Laval, 1971. 5 reels.

    QSHERU   mfm   (L)

622. Victoria and Albert Museum, London. Dept. of Prints and Drawings. <u>Architectural Drawings in the Victoria and Albert Museum</u>. East Ardsley, Wakefield, Micro Methods Ltd. 23 reels.

    OKQ   mfm   (LP)

623. Voltaire, Francois Marie Arouet de. <u>Oeuvres Completes Nouv. ed.</u> 52 v. 1877-85. Washington: Microcard Editions, 1966. 365 cards.

    OGU   mcd   OSUL   mcd   (L)

    Guide: Volume 51-52; Table Generale et Analytique des Matieres Contenues dans les Oeuvres de Voltaire. (mfe)

624. Webster, Daniel. <u>Papers</u>. Ann Arbor, Mich., University Microfilms in Colloboration with Dartmouth College Library, Hanover, N.H., 1871. 41 reels.

    OWA   mfm   (LP)

    Guide: <u>Guide and Index to the Microfilm</u>, Charles M. Wiltse, ed. Ann Arbor, Mich., 1971.

625. Wenck, Friedrich August Wilhelm. <u>Codex Juris Gentium Recentissimi</u>, 1781-1795, 3 v. Washington, D.C., Microcard Editions. 44 fiche.

    QLB   mfe   (L)

626. Westminster Cathedral. Archives. <u>Westminster Cathedral Archives, Series A</u>. East Ardsley, Wakefield, Yorkshire, Micro Methods, 1965. 46 reels.

    OWA   mfm   (LP)

627. Wisconsin, State Historical Society. <u>Collection of Communist Pamphlets, 1929-1949</u>. Madison, Wisconsin 1972? 3 reels.

    QMG   mfm   (L)

628. Wittgenstein, Ludwig. The Wittgenstein Papers. Ithaca, N.Y., Photo Science of Cornell University, 1968. 20 reels. With printed index. Manuscripts and papers from the Library of Trinity College, Cambridge, and in private hands.

   OTU   mfm   (LP)   QMM   mfm   (P)
   QMG   mfm   (L)

629. Wolfenbuettel. Herzog-August-Bibliothek. Libretti. Nendeln, Liechtenstein, Kraus - Thomson Organization, 1971?

   OTU   mfe

      Guide: Wolfenbuettel. Herzog-August-Bibliothek. Katalog. Frankfurt am Main, V. Klostermann, 1970.

630. Women and/in Health. Filmed by Women's History Research Center. -- Berkeley, Calif., Women's History Research Center, 1974. 13 reels.

   OHM   mfm   (LP)

      Guide: Guide to the Microfilm Edition of the Women and Health Collection. Berkeley, Calif., Women's History Research Center.

631. Woolf, Virginia Stephen. Orlando; MS from Knole Kent. Wakefield, Yorks, Micro Methods Ltd. 1 reel.

   OTR   mfm   (L)

632. World Council of Churches. Commission on Faith and Order. Official Publications, 1910-1962. Fort Worth, Texas, Texas Christian University, 1954-   6 reels.

   OHM   mfm   (LP)   QMM   mfm   (P)

633. World Health Organization. World Health. Washington, D.C., NCR Microcard Editions. 59 fiche.

   OSUL   mfe   (1966-69)   (L)

634. Zarlino, Gioseffo. De Tutte l'Opere del R.M. Gioseffo Zarlino da Chioggia. Venetia, Francesco de Franceschi Senese, 1588-89. 4 v. Zug, Inter Documentation Co. 1972. 35 fiche.

   OWA   mfe   (L)

	Item No.
Abstracts of the Proceedings of the Council of the Governor General of India Assembled for the Purpose of Making Laws and Regulations...	317
Acta Sanctae Sedis, v.1-41: 1863-1908...................................	1
Acts of the Privy Council of England...................................	270
Acts of the Privy Council of England, Colonial Series, 1613-1783........	271
The Adams Papers Owned by the Adams Manuscript Trust and Deposited in the Massachusetts Historical, 1639-1889............................	2
Adelphi Papers, no.1- . 1963..	3
Agardh, Jacob Georg. Analecta Algologica: Observations de Speciebus Algarum Minus Cognitis Earumque Disposititione, Continuatio I. 1894-	4
Agricultural Information on Mainland China, 1953-1967...................	566
Ajia Keizai Kenkyujo, Tokyo. Economic Development and Planning of Asian and African Countries..	5
Ajia Keizai Kenkyujo, Tokyo. Trade Statistics of Asian Countries........	6,7
Allgemeine Deutsche Biographie, 1875-1912...............................	8
Allied Powers Reparation Commission. Reparation Papers of the Allied Powers Reparation Commission, 1922-1930............................	9
Almanach National; Annuaire Officiel de la Republique Francaise, 1770-1879...	10
Alphabetisches Hauptregister uber die Protokolle der Deutschen Bundesversammlung...	214
Alphabetisches Register uber die Verhandlungen der Deutschen Bundesversammlung...	214
America and West Indies, Original Correspondence etc. 1606-1808.........	236
American Bibliography; A Preliminary Checklist for 1801-1819............	163
American Bibliography ... 1639 Down to and Including the Year 1820......	162
American Colonial Records; Records for the 18th and 19th Centuries in 15 Eastern States..	11
American Culture Series, 1493-1806......................................	12
American Fiction. Ser.1: 1774-1850; Ser.2: 1851-1875; Ser.3: 1876-1900	18
American Film Institute. Edwin B. Hayes Oral History Collection........	408
American Historical Association. Committee for the Study of War Documents. A Catalogue of Files and Microfilms of the German Foreign Ministry Archives 1867-1920................................	218
American Literature of the 19th Century.................................	14
American Loyalist Claims...	240,241
American Periodicals Series..	15,16
American Periodicals Series. A Consolidated Index to the Microfilm Series of the 18th Century Periodicals and to the First 10 years of the 1800-1850 Series...	16
American Prose Fiction 1774-1900 Cumulative Author Index................	13
American State Papers, 1789-1838, Serial Set, 15th Congress 1817........	557
Analecta Algologica: Observationes de Speciebus Algarum Minus Cognitis Earumque Disposititione, Sontinuatio I. 1894..............	4
Angela Davis Case Collection...	143
Angotti, V.L. Source Materials in the Field of Theatre, an Annotated Bibliography and Subject Guide to the Microfilm Collection........	517
Annotated Catalogue of the Papers of Charles S. :eirce.................	438

107

                                                                    Item No.

Annotated Proofs of the Works of Charles Dickens From the Forster
    Collection in the Victoria and Albert Museum........................ 151
Annual Report on the Colonies, 1889-1939................................ 237
Architectural Drawings in the Victoria and Albert Museum................ 622
Archiv Kniazîa Voront'sova Moscow, 1870-1895............................ 17
Archives de la Linguistique Francaise; Collection de Documents
    Relatifs a la Langue Francaise, Publiees Entre 1500 et 1900
    Paris, France - Expansion, 1972..............1...................... 18
Archives de la Rochelle (France). S.L.Archives Départmentales
    de la Charente-Maritime... 19
Archives Deplomatiques, Correspondance Consulaire D'Odessa.
    Ministère des Affaires Etrangères, 1802-20.......................... 20
Archives Diplomatiques; Recueil Mensuel de Diplomatic D'histoire et
    de Droit International.. 21
Archives of British Men of Science: A Survey of Private and
    Institutional Holdings of British Scientific Archives............... 376
Archives Parlementaires de 1787 a 1860: Recueil complet des Debats
    Legislatifs & Politiques de Chambres Francaises..................... 22
Armaments Yearbook. Category IX. 1924-1940.............................. 355
Art Exhibition Catalogues Republished on Microfiche..................... 23
Association of Research Libraries. Center for Chinese Research
    Materials. Chinese Maritime Customs Publications. Chung-Kuo
    Hai-Kuan Chu'u-Pan P'in 1860-1948................................... 24
Association Universitaire Pour la Diffusion Internationale dela
    Recherche. Bibliotheque de Recherche. Etudes de Sinologie........... 25
Austin, Robert E. Early American Medical Imprints: A Guide Printed
    in the United States, 1668-1820..................................... 164
Australia. Royal Commission on Australian Government Administration.
    Collected Papers of the Royal Commission on Australian
    Government Administration, 1974..................................... 26
Behavioural Science Notes... 313
Bergquist, G. William, ed. Three Centuries of, English and American
    Plays, a Checklist. England: 1500-1800; United States
    1714-1830... 534
Berlin(West Berlin) Allied Kommandatura. Official Gazette of the
    Allied Kommandatura Berlin.. 27
Bible N.T. Gospels. Greek. Gospels in Greek 11th Century................ 28
Bible O.T. Pentateuch. Judeo-Persian. 1973. Biblia Judaeo-Persica....... 29
Bibliografia de Literatura Hispanica Madrid............................. 305
Bibliography and Reel Index. A Guide to the Microfilm Edition of
    International Population Census Publications 1945-67................ 325
Bibliography of American Culture, 1439-1875............................. 12
A Bibliography of Canadiana, (1534-1867) in the Toronto Public
    Library; Edited by Frances M.Staton and Marie Tremaine.............. 99
A Bibliography of French Plays on Microcards............................ 535
Bibliography of French Revolutionary Pamphlets on Microfiche............ 203
A Bibliography of German Plays on Microcards............................ 215
A Bibliography of Kentucky History...................................... 339
A Bibliography of Spanish Plays on Microcards........................... 192

Item No.

A Bibliography of the Frank E. Melvin Collection of Pamphlets of
    the French Revolution in the University of Kansas Libraries..... 203
A Bibliography of the Prairie Provinces to 1953........................ 437
Bibliotheca Americana: A Dictionary of Books Relating to America
    from its Discovery to the Present Time. 29 vols. 1868-1936....... 335
Binger, Norman. A Bibliography of German Plays on Microcards......... 215
Boccaccio, Giovanni. Decameron.. 30
Bond, Richmond P. Studies in the Early English Periodical............ 177
Books Printed in the Netherlands and Belgium Before 1601.............. 31
Borden, (Sir) Robert Laird. The Borden Papers, 1893-1937............. 32
Borden, (Sir) Robert Laird. Diary of Sir Robert Borden: Washington
    Disarmament Conference 1921-1922.................................. 33
The Borden Papers, 1893-1937.. 32
Boucher, Pierre. Fonds Boucher. Seigneurie Boucherville a
    Concessions 1716-20... 34
Bourassa, Henri. Articles de Henri Bourassa Publiés dans le Devoir.. 35
Bourassa, Henri. Papiers de Henri Bourassa et Sa Correspondance..... 36
Brimmer, Brenda et al. A Guide to the Use of U.N. Documents.......... 547
Bristol, Roger P. Supplement to Chas. Evans' American Bibliography... 162
Britain and Europe Since 1945... 37
British and Continental Rhetoric and Elocution........................ 38
British and Foreign State Papers 1812................................. 244
British Birth Control Material at the British Library of Political
    and Economic Sciences: 1800-1957.................................. 39
British Cabinet Papers on Microfilm, 1902-1945........................ 40
British Columbia, British Columbia Gazette............................ 41
British Columbia. Laws, Statutes, etc. Revised Statutes, 1871-1897.. 42
British Columbia. Legislative Assembly. Journals, 1872-1903......... 43
British Columbia. Legislative Assembly. Sessional Papers,1876-1903. 44
British Conservative Party. Archives of the British Conservative
    Party. Pamphlets and Leaflets, Ser.1, 1868-1914.................. 45
British Culture Series; a Selection of Books Relating to English
    Culture of the 18th and 19th Centuries............................ 46
British Labour History Ephemera. Pamphlets, 1-1159, 1900-1926....... 47
British Labour Party. Archives of the British Labour Party.
    Pamphlets and Leaflets, Ser.1, 1900-1959. Ser.2, 1900-1926....... 48
British Museum. Dept. of Printed Books. Short-title Catalogue of
    Books Printed in France and of French Books Printed in Other
    countries From 1470-1600.. 201
British Museum. Dept. of Printed Books. Short-title Catalogue of
    Books Printed in Other Countries From 1465-1600................... 327
British Museum. Dept. of Printed Books. Short-title Catalogue of
    Books Printed in Spain and of Spanish Books Printed Elsewhere
    in Europe Before 1601... 305
British Museum. Dept. of Printed Books. Short-title Catalogue of
    Books Printed in the German-speaking Countries From
    1455 to 1600.. 212

	Item No.

British Museum. Dept. of Printed Books. Short-title Catalogue of Books Printed in the Netherlands and Belgium and of Dutch and Flemish Books ... 1470-1600 Now in the British Museum............. 31
British Museum. Dept. of Printed Books. Thomason Collection. Catalogue of Pamphlets Books, Newspapers, and Manuscripts Relating the Civil War, the Commonwealth and Restoration.......... 533
British Records Relating to America in Microform..................... 49
British Sessional Papers.. 264-266
British Trade Union History Collection: Major Works on the Trade Unions and Their leaders from Their Inception to the Present Day. 50
Buchez, Phillippe J. Histoire Parlementaire de la Révolution Française.. 51
Burghley, William Cecil, Baron. Politics and Administration of Tudor England: Lord Burghley's Papers in the British Library in London. 52
CAN/FIL; Canadian Financial Information Library....................... 53
CANEDEX. Canadian Education Monographs on Microfiche.................. 54
CIS/Index to Publications of the United States Congress............... 127
CIS Microfiche Library. 1976... 127
Cabinet Reports From Prime Ministers to the Crown 1868-1916........... 233
Calendar of Letters and State Papers Foreign and Domestic. Henry VIII, 1509-1545... 273
Calendar of State Papers... 274
Calendar of State Papers, Colonial Series, 1574-1733................. 275
Calendar of State Papers, Domestic Series, Charles I. 1625-1649....... 276
Calendar of State Papers, Domestic Series, Charles II 1660-1670....... 277
Calendar of State Papers, Domestic Series. The Commonwealth, 1649-1660... 278
Calendar of State Papers, Domestic Series. Edward VI, Mary Elizabeth I. James I, 1547-1625. 12 vols......................... 279
Calendar of State Papers, Domestic Series. William III, 1689-95...... 280
Calendar of State Papers, Foreign Series. Edward VI, 1547-1553 Mary 1553-1558, Elizabeth I, 1558-1582, 18 vols................... 281
Calendar of the Court Minutes etc. of the East India Company.......... 167
California. Governor's Commission on the Los Angeles Riots. Transcripts Depositions, Consultant's Reports, and Selected Documents. 1965... 55
Calvin, John. Opera Quae Supersunt Omnia, 1863-1900.................. 56
Camden Society London. Publications................................. 57,58
Canada. Census. Census of Canada, 1971, Maps in Enumeration Area Series.. 60
Canada. Census. Census Returns...................................... 59
Canada. Commission of Inquiry Into the Non-Medical Use of Drugs. Index to Briefs and Transcripts of Hearings....................... 75
Canada. Department of Indian Affairs. Annual.Report, 1880-1936...... 61
Canada. Department of Indian Affairs and Northern Development. National Parks Bibliographies..................................... 62
Canada. Federal Provincial Conferences. Documents From Federal Provincial Conferences in Canada, 1887-1976...................... 63

	Item No.
Canada. Parliament. House of Commons. Canadian Parliamentary Proceedings and Sessional Papers. 1841-1970.....................	64
Canada. Parliament House of Commons, Debates (Reported in Newspapers) 1846-1874..	65
Canada. Parliament. House of Commons. General Index to the House of Commons, 1867-1930...	66
Canada. Parliament. House of Commons. Journals, 1867-1970..........	66
Canada. Parliament. House of Commons. Sessional Papers of the Dominion of Canada. 1867-1925.......................................	67
Canada. Parliament. House of Commons. Standing and Special Committees. Reports and Minutes of Proceedings and Evidence, 1935-1970..	68
Canada. Parliament. House of Commons. Unpublished Sessional Papers, 1916-1958..	69
Canada. Parliament. Library. English Language Card Catalogue, 1976.	
Canada. Parliament. Senate. Special Committee on Mass Media Briefs, 1970...	71
Canada. Public Archives. Archives Canada Microfiches...............	72
Canada. Public Archives. Catalogue of Pamphlets in the Public Archives of Canada Prepared by Magdalon Casey......................	74
Canada. Public Archives. Centennial Issues of Canadian Newspapers...	73
Canada. Public Archives. The Laurier Papers: Author Index; Subject Index...	354
Canada. Public Archives. Pamphlets in tne Public Archives, 1493-1877..	74
Canada. Royal Commission of Inquiry Into the Non-Medical Use of Drugs, 1972. Briefs and Transcripts.............................	75
Canada. Royal Commission of Inquiry Into the Non-Medical Use of Drugs. Research Papers...	76
Canada. Royal Commission on Bilingualism and Biculturalism. Briefs and Transcripts. 1972..	77
Canada. Royal Commission on Bilingualism and Biculturalism. Index to Briefs and Transcripts of Public Hearings......................	77
Canada. Royal Commission on Bilingualism and Biculturalism. Research Studies...	78
Canada. Royal Commission on Broadcasting, 1956. Briefs and Transcripts...	79
Canada. Royal Commission on Canada's Economic Prospects, 1955-1957. Briefs and Transcripts of Public Hearings.........................	80
Canada. Royal Commission on Canada's Economic Prospects. Index to Briefs and Transcripts of Public Hearings.........................	80
Canada. Royal Commission on Dominion-Provincial Relations. Briefs and Transcripts..	81
Canada. Royal Commission on Dominion-Provincial Relations. Index to Briefs and Transcripts of Public Hearings......................	81
Canada. Royal Commission on Energy. Briefs and Transcripts..........	82
Canada. Royal Commission on National Development in the Arts, Letters and Sciences. Index to Briefs and Transcripts of Public Hearings..	83

	Item No.
Canada. Royal Commission on National Development in the Arts, Letters and Sciences 1949-1951. Briefs and Transcripts....................	83
Canada. Royal Commission on Taxation. Briefs 1962....................	84
Canada. Royal Commission on Taxation. Index to Briefs and Transcripts of Public Hearings......................................	84
Canada. Royal Commission on the Status of Women. Briefs and Transcripts..	85
Canada. Royal Commission on the Status of Women. Index to Briefs and Transcripts of Public Hearings..................................	88
Canada. Royal Commission on the Status of Women. Studies............	86
Canada (Province). Department of Public Instruction for Upper Canada. Journal of Education for Upper Canada. 1848-1867.........	87
Canada (Province). Parliament. Legislative Assembly. General Index to the Journals of the Legislative Assembly of Canada, 1852-66...	88
Canada (Province). Parliament. Legislative Assembly. Journals of the Legislative Assembly 1842-1866; Appendix to the Journals, 1842-1859; Sessional Papers, 1860-1866..............................	88
Canada (Province). Parliament. Legislative Council. Index to the Journals of the Legislative Council. 13 vols....................	89
Canada (Province). Parliament. Legislative Council. Journals, v.1-26, 1841-1866...	89
Canadian Education Monographs on Microfiche.........................	54
Canadian Federal Royal Commission Reports, 1867-1966.................	90
Canadian Historical Documents. Part One. Quebec Literary and Historical Society Documents (1838-1915); Part Three Documents From the Canadian Public Archives (1882-1902)...........	91
Canadian Imprints. 1751-1800. Identified by Tremaine Nunbers; Reproductions of Items Listed in Marie Tremain's A Bibliography of Canadian Inprints, 1751-1800......................	92
Canadian Library Association. Microfilm Committee. Canadian Newspapers on Microfilm, a Catalogue.............................	93
Canadian Library Association. Newspaper Microfilming Project. Canadian Newspapers on Microfilm..................................	93
Canadian Music Centre, Toronto. Collection of Unpublished Canadian Music Scores..	94
Canadian Newspapers on Microfilm....................................	93
Canadian Northwest..	95
Canadian Parliamentary Proceedings and Sessional Papers, 1841-1970....	64
Canadian Publications in the Field of Urban and Regional Planning and Development...	96
Canadian Theses on Microfiche/Microfilm.............................	97
Canadian Theses on Microfilm Catalogue..............................	97
Canadian Urban Sources, 1973-75.....................................	98
Canadian Urban Sources. Table of Contents, Listing by Microfiche Accession Number..	98
Canadiana...	97
Canadiana in the Toronto Public Library.............................	99

                                                                    Item No.

Canney, Margaret, and Knott, David. Catalogue of the Goldsmith's
    Library of Economic Literature:................................. 225
Carleton, Sir Guy. Historical, Military Records of the British Army
    in the American Revolution, 1747-1783............................ 100
Carlyle, Thomas. Correspondence of Thomas Carlyle and Mrs. Jane
    Carlyle From Carlyle's House, 24 Cheyne Row, Chelsea............. 101
Carnegie-Myrdal Study: The Negro in America: Research Emoranda For Use
    in the Preparation of Dr. Gunnar Myrdal's An American Dilemma.... 102
Catalog of Selected Documents on the Disadvantaged (ERIC Educational
    Documents Index, 1966-1969)...................................... 584
Catalogue Cards in Book Form for United States Joint Publications
    Research Service Translations.................................... 589
Catalogue of a Collection of Historical Tracts, 1561-1800............. 306
Catalogue of Files and Microfilms of the German Foreign Ministry
    Archives 1867-1920... 218
Catalogue of Italian Plays 1500-1700 in the Library of the University
    of Toronto... 328
Catalogue of Microfiche Series of Political Literature of Northern
    Ireland 1968-72: Subject and Alphabetical Listings............... 412
Catalogue of Microfiche Series of Political Literature of Northern
    Ireland 1973-74 and 1975: Subject and Alphabetical Listings...... 412
Catalogue of Microfilms of Unpublished Canadian Music................. 94
Catalogue of Pamphlets, Books, Newspapers and Manuscripts Relating the
    Civil War, the Commonwealth and Restoration, Collected by
    George Thomason 1640-1661.. 533
Catalogue of Pamphlets in the Public Archives of Canada, Prepared by
    Magdalon Casey... 74
Catalogue of the Goldsmiths' Library of Economic Literature: With an
    Introduction by J.H.P. Pafford................................... 225
Catalogue of the Library of the Peabody Institute of the City of
    Baltimore.. 397, 398
Catalogue of the Petrarch Collection in Cornell University Library.... 130
Catalogue of the United States Census Publications 1790-1945.......... 550
Catholic Church. Congregation de Propaganda Fide, Acts, 1622-1862..... 103
Catholic Church in France. Assemblée Générale du Clergé.
    Collection des Procès-Verbaux des Assemblées-Générales du Clergé
    de France Depuis L'Année 1560 Jusqu'à Présent.................... 104
Census of Canada, 1971, Maps in Enumeration Area Series............... 60
Census of India 1871/72-1951.. 320
Challen, William Harold, Comp. Parish Register Typescripts.
    Prepared by W.H. Challen From Parishes in London................. 105
Charente-Maritime, France (Dept.) Archives Departmentales. Documents
    Appartenant Aux Archives Departmentales de la Gironde............ 106
The Charles S. Peirce Papers.. 438
Chatham Newspapers, 1848-1942... 107
Chaucer, Geoffrey. Chaucer Manuscripts; Manly Collection in
    University of Chicago Libraries.................................. 108
Chaucer Society, London. Publications, Ser. 1 and 2................... 109
Checklist of Additions to Evans' American Bibliography in the Rare
    Book Division.. 162

	Item No.
Checklist of American Drama Published in the English Colonies of North America and the United States....................................	173
Checklist of Courtesy Books in the Newberry Library, Compiled by Virgil B. Heltzel..	409
Checklist of French Political Pamphlets, 1560-1644 in the Newberry Library...	410
Checklist of the Writings of Daniel Defoe............................	146
Checklist of United Nations Documents................................	547
Ch'en, Ch'eng. Shih-Sou Tzu Liao Shih Kung Fei Tzu Liao..............	110
Chicago, University of (Theses, Ph.D) Chicago, University of Chicago Library, Dept. of Photographic Reproduction 1934?-1947...........	111
China. Inspectorate General of Customs. Decennial Reports on the Trade, Navigation, Industries, etc. of the Ports Open to Foreign Commerce in China and Corea, and on the Condition and Development of the Treaty Port Provinces....................................	112
China and Asia (Exclusive of Near East). Bibliography-Index to U.S. JPRS Research Translations......................................	589
Chinese Communism 1927-1964: A Collection of Pamphlets Issued by Chinese Communist Leaders and Party Officials...................	113
Chinese Culture Series...	114
Chinese Maritime Customs Publications Chung-Kuo Hai-Kuan Ch'u-Pan P'in 1860-1948...	24
Chronological Index to the Diplomatic Correspondence of British Ministers to the Russian Court at St. Petersburg 1704-1776.......	155
Church Missionary Society. Proceedings of the Church Missionary Society for Africa and the East. London, 1801-1921.............	115
Church Missionary Society. Records Relating to Africa, Circa 1803-1904/21...	116
Church Missionary Society. West Indies Mission Records, 1819-1861....	117
Church Missionary Society. Yoruba Mission; Niger Mission; South African Mission; East African Mission; Nyanza Mission; Kenya Mission...	118
Church of Geneva. Ecclesiastical Correspondence......................	119
Clare, John. Manuscripts From the Collection in Northampton Central Library...	120
Clark, Thomas D. Travels in the New South; a Bibliography............	540
Clark, Thomas D. Travels in the Old South; a Bibliography............	541
Claude Kitchin Papers in the Southern Historical Collection of the University of North Carolina Library.............................	121
Clubb, Louise George. Italian Plays (1500-1700)in the Folger Library: A Bibliography with Introduction.......................	328
Codex Juris Gentium Recentissimi.....................................	625
Colbert, Jean-Baptiste, 1619-1683. Lettres, Instruction set memoires de Colbert..	122
Coleman, J.E. A Bibliography of Kentucky History....................	339
Collected Correspondence and Miscellaneous Papers of David Garrick....	207
Collected Papers of the Royal Commission on Australian Government Administration, 1974...	26
Collection Adrien Arcanda..	123
Collection D'articles De M. André Laurendeau Parus Dans Le Devoir 1947-1967...	353

	Item No.
Collection Des Procès-Verbaus Des Assemblées-Générales Du Clergé De France Depuis L'Année 1560 Jusqu'à Présent	104
Collection Music Department Haags Gemeentemuseum	293
Collection of Agricultural Information on Mainland China, 1948-1967	567
Collection of Communist Pamphlets	627
Collection of Hungarian Political and Military Records, 1909-1945	594
A Collection of Scarce and Valuable Tracts on the Most Entertaining Subjects. 1809-1815	502
Collection of Targum Manuscrips and Fragments	124
The Collection of the Honourable Louis Arthur Grimes, 1883-1948	291
Collection of Unpublished Canadian Musical Scores	94
La Collezione Palatina (de Commedia, Drammi, Pastorali, Tragedie e Drammi Spirituali, Tragicommedie e di Pescatorie e Marittime)	190
Colonial Numbered Series, 1924-60	242
Columbia University Oral History Collection	408
Communist Party of Great Britain. Publications	125
Community Cross-Reference Guide to Phonefiche: Current Telephone Directories on Microfiche	442
A Complete List of the Names of the Authors Whose Works are Printed in the Greek Series of Migne's Patrologia	398
Condition Ouvrière en France au 19e Siècle	126
Cone Tanjur. 209v	529
Confidential Print on China, 1848-1937	246
Confidential Prints on China and the Far East, 1857-1915	247
Congregation de Propaganda Fide, Acta, 1622-1862	103
Congressional Globe. Twenty-Third Congress, Dec.2, 1833, Forty-Second Congress, March 3, 1873	560
Congressional Information Service. CIS Microfiche Library. 1976-	127
Congressional Record, Forty-Third Congress, Dec.1, 1873	561
A Consolidated Guide to Segment 1 of the Microfilm Collection	225
Conspectus Auctorum Quorum Nomina Indicibus Patrologiae Graeco-Latinae a J.P. Migne Editae Continentur	398
Consular Despatches, 1790-1906	568
Conti, Antonio Schinella. Selected Works; a Selection of 11 MSS. From the Biblioteca Comunale Vincenzo Joppi di Udine	128
Cook, James. Log and Journal of Captain Cook's Voyage Round the World in the Bark "Endeavour" 1768-1771	129
Cook, Lawson, ed. Musicache: Index Fiche 1-1002	404
Cook, Lawson, ed. Musicache: Indexing System	404
Cornell University. Petrarch Collection	130
Cornell University. Olin Library. The Cornell University Collection of Women's Rights pamphlets, 1814-1912	131
Corps Universel Diplomatique du Droit Des Gens. 1726-	161
Corpus Scriptorum Ecclesiaticorum Latinorum. Vols.1-60, 1866-1913	132
Correspondance de Henri Bourassa Avec Laurier Sir Wilfred, Lavergne Armand	133
Correspondence of Thomas Carlyle and Mrs. Jane Carlyle From Carlyle's House, 24 Cheyne Row, Chelsea	101
Correspondence with Her Majesty's Envoy Extraordinary Minister Plenipotentiary in Japan, August 1859-1910	248

Item No.

Corrigan, Beatrice. Catalogue of Italian Plays 1500-1700 in the Library of the University of Toronto................................	328
Courtesy Books, 1571-1773...	409
Covent Garden Prompt Books..	134
Crick, B.R. and Miriam Alman, eds. A Guide to Manuscripts Relating to America in Great Britain and Ireland.............................	49
Crime and Juvenile Delinquency..	135
Crime and Juvenile Delinquency: a Preliminary Checklist of the Titles in the Basic Collection...	135
Cuba. Laws, Statutes, etc. Gaceta Oficial de la Republica de Cuba. April 1902-Oct. 1967...	136
Current National Statistical Compendiums, 1970-73.....................	137
Cyrillic Union Catalogue..	591
Daly's Fifth Avenue Theatre, New York. Bill of the Play; 1879-1892, 1896-97..	138
Daly's Fifth Avenue Theatre, Collection of Programs, 1879-1899........	139
Daly's Fifth Avenue Theatre. New York. Correspondence and Documents, 1858-1899..	140
Daly's Fifth Avenue Theatre. New York. Scrapbooks, 1863-1899..........	141
Dante Alighieri. Divina Comedia......................................	142
Davis, Angela Yvonne. Angela Davis Case Collection...................	143
De tutte l'opere del R.M. Gioseffo Zarlino da Chioggia...............	634
The Debates and Proceedings in the Congress of the U.S., First Session, March 3, 1789 - Eighteenth Session, May 27, 1824.........	562
Decennial Reports on the Trade, Navigation, Industries, etc of the Ports Open to Foreign Commerce in China and Corea, and on the Conditions and Development of the Treaty Port Provinces...........	112
The Declassified Documents Quarterly Catalogue. (Abstracts and Cumulative Subject Index)..	144
The Declassified Documents Reference System. Annual Collection........	144
The Declassified Documents Reference System. Retrospective Collection.	145
The Declassified Documents Reference System. Retrospective Collection. Catalogue of Abstracts...	145
Defoe, Daniel. The Writings of Daniel Defoe..........................	146
De Groot, A.I., ed. Library of Church Unity Periodicals. Ser.1-3.....	147
Despatches From United States Consuls, Hamilton, Ont. 1867-1906.......	569
Despatches From United States Ministers to China, 1843-1906...........	570
Despatches From United States Ministers to Great Britain 1791-1906....	571
Development Plans (Social and Economic Development Plans. D101-859)...	148
D'Holbach et ses amis, 1760-1789......................................	149
The Diaries of Henry Scadding...	498
Diary of Sir Robert Borden: Washington Disarmament Conference 1921-1922...	33
Dibdin, Thomas John. The London Theatre; a Collection of the Most Celebrated Dramatic Pieces.......................................	150
Dickens, Charles. Annotated Proofs of the Works of Charles Dickens From the Forster Collection in the Victoria and Albert Museum....	151
Dickens, Charles. Manuscripts of the Works of Charles Dickens From the Forster Collection in the Victoria and Albert Museum.........	152
Dickens, Charles. Original Letters of Charles Dickens in the Dickens House..	153

	Item No.
Dickens, Charles. Original Manuscripts of Charles Dickens and Other Papers	154
Diplomatic Correspondence of British Ministers to the Russian Court at St. Petersburg 1704-1776	155
Diplomatic Instructions of the Department of State, 1801-1906	572
Documentary History of the Ratification of the Constitution. Edited by Merrill Jensen	156
Documents Appartenant Aux Archives Departmentales da la Gironde	106
Documents de la Session du Quebec, 1867-1972	459
Documents diplomatiques francais, 1871-1914	197
Documents From Federal Provincial Conferences in Canada, 1887-1976	63
Documents From the Canadian Public Archives, 1882-1902	91
Dod's Parliamentary Companion	158,159
Dodsley, Robert, Comp. A Select Collection of Old English Plays	160
Dubester, Henry J., Catalogue of the United States Census Publications 1790-1945	534
Dumont, Jean. Corps Universel Diplomatique du droit des gens. 1726-1731	161
Early American Imprints, First Series, 1639-1800, Clifford K. Shipton Evans no. 1-	162
Early American Imprints, Second Series (Shaw-Shoemaker), 1801-1819	168
Early American Medical Imprints, 1668-1820	164
Early American Newspapers, 1704-1820	208
Early English Books. See English Books	174,175
Early English Text Society Publications, Original Series. Nos. 1-47	165
Early Toronto Planning Documents	166
East Europe; Bibliography-Index to U.S. JPRS Research Translations	589
East India Company. A Calendar of the Court Minutes etc. of the East India Company, 1635-79	167
Ecclesiastical Correspondence	119
Economic Development and Planning of Asian and African Countries	5
Economic Working Papers	168
Educational Testing Service. Tests in Microfiche	169
Eighteenth Century Russian Publications	171,403
Eighteenth Century Sources for the Study of English Literature	172
Elucidation in 235 Tabulas Patrologiae Latinae Auctore Cartusiensi	398
English and American Drama of the 19th Century; American Plays, 1831-1900. English Plays, 1801-1900	173
English Books, 1475-1640	175
English Books, 1641-1700	175
English Experience, Group 1-10	176
The English Factories in India; a Calendar of Documents in India Office, British Museum and Public Record Office	191
English Literary Periodicals 17th, 18th, and 19th Centuries. A guide to the Contents	177
English Literary Periodicals, 1600-1900	177
English Reports. Full Reprint	178
Envirofiche	179

	Item No.
Environment Abstracts	179
Eric Documents	585
Essai sur la Musique Ancienne et Moderne	343
Ethnographic Atlas	313
European Official Statistical Serials on Space Microfiche, 1846-1965	180
Evangelical Academies and Lay Training Centers of Europe and Great Britain. Historical Sketches, Conference Programs	181
Evans, (Sir) Arthur John. Evans and Mackenzie Note Books, 1900-1929	182
Evans, Charles. American Bibliography...1639 Down to and Including the Year 1820	162
Evans and Mackenzie Note Books, 1900-1929	182
FLQ. Clipping from Canadian Newspapers and Magazines, 1970-1971	183
Faber du Faur, Curt von. German Baroque Literature: A Catalogue of the Collection in the Yale University Library	211
Fabian Society, London. Minute Books, 1884-1918	184
Fabian Society Tracts, 1884-1942	185
Facsimiles of Manuscripts in European Archives Relating to America, 1773-1783	525
Faillon, Etienne Michel. Fonds Faillon. Index 1677-1834	186
Federal Population Censuses, 1790-1890	552
Files of Evidence Connected with the Investigation of the Assassination of President John F. Kennedy	187
Finney Papers, 1792-1875	188
Finnish-Canadian Play and Operetta Manuscript Collection	189
Finnish Organization of Canada. Finnish-Canadian Play and Operetta Manuscript Collection	189
Fliegel, Rev. Carl John. Index to the Records of the Moravian Mission Among the Indians of North America	402
Florence. Biblioteca Nazionale Centrale. La Collezione Palatina (de Commedia, Drammi, Pastorali, Tragedie e Drammi Spirituali, Tragicommedie e di Pescatorie e Marittime)	190
Fonds Boucher. Seigneurie Boucherville a Concessions, 1716-20	34
Fonds Faillon. Index 1677-1834	186
Fonds Verreau: du Carton I au Carton IX	621
Ford Percy. A Guide to Parliamentary Papers, What They are, How to Find Them	266
Foreign Office Confidential Papers Relating to China and Her Neighbouring Countries, 1840-1914, With an Additional List 1915-1937	247
Foreign Office Records and Consular Reports From the Ottoman Empire	282
Foster, Sir William. The English Factories in India; a Calendar of Documents in India Office, British Museum and Public Record Office	191
Four Centuries of Spanish Drama: 1500-1900	192
France. Journal Officiel de la Republique Francaise, 1869-1880	193
France. Journal Officiel de la République Française sous la Commune 1871 Paris	194
France. Assemblée Nationale 1871-1942. Chambre des Deputes. Débats Parlementaires, 1881-1940	195

                                                                    Item No.

France. Assemblée Nationale Chambre des Deputés. Documents
  Parlementaires, Sessions Ordinaires: 1881-1938. Sessions
  Extraordinaires... 196
France. Commission de Publication des Documents Relatifs aux
  Origines de la Guerre de 1914. Documents Diplomatiques
  Français, (1871-1914).. 197
France. Conseil des Depêches. Repertoire Chronologique et Analytique
  des Arrêts du Conseil des Depêches 1611-1710................... 198
France. Ministre de l'Agriculture et du Commerce. Annuaire
  Statistique. 1878-1965... 199
Franklin Institute, Philadelphia. Committee on Science and the Arts..
  Records of the Committee on Science and the Arts of the
  Franklin Institute, 1824-1900.................................. 200
French Books Before 1601... 201
French Political Pamphlets, 1560-1653, From Collections in the
  Newberry Library... 410
French Revolutionary Materials, Maclure Collection, Univ. of
  Pennsylvania... 202
French Revolutionary Pamphlets on Microcards..................... 203
Fritsch, Felix Eugene. Fritsch Collection of Algae............... 204
Fritsch Collection of Algae...................................... 204
The Fulham Papers in Lambeth Palace Library; American Colonial
  Section Calendar and Indexes................................... 349
Gaceta Oficial de la Republica de Cuba. April 1902-Oct.1967...... 136
Gallatin, Albert. The Papers of Albert Gallatin.................. 205
Garden, Guillaume de. Histoire Générale des Traites de Paix et
  Autres Transactions Principales Entre Toutes les Puissances de
  l'Europe Depuis la Paix de Westphalie.......................... 206
Garrick, David. Collected Correspondence and Miscellaneous Papers of
  David Garrick.. 207
Gaustad, E.S. Religion in America: an Annotated Bibliography of
  Selected Dissertations... 471
Gaustad, E.S. Religion in America: Early Books and Manuscripts: an
  Annotated Bibliography and Guide to the Microfilm Collection... 472
Gay, Ebenezer, ed. Early American Newspapers, 1704-1820.......... 209
General Correspondence Before 1906. Archives of Conferences,
  1813-1822.. 251
General Correspondence Before 1906. China 1815-1850.............. 252
General Correspondence Before 1906, Continent Conferences, 1814-
  1822... 253
General Correspondence Before 1906, Slave Trade 1816-1892........ 254
General Correspondence Before 1906, United States of America Series 1,
  1782-1795.. 255
General Index to the House of Commons, 1867-1930................. 66
General Index to the Journals of the Legislative Assembly of Canada,
  1852-66.. 88
The German Army High Command, 1938-1945.......................... 209
German Baroque Literature. Harold Jantz Collection............... 210
German Baroque Literature: A Catalogue of the Collection in the Yale
  university Library.   211

                                119

Item No.

German Baroque Literature; a Descriptive Catalogue and Guide to the Collection on Microfilm..	210
German Baroque Literature; Yale University Collection................	211
German Books Before 1601...	212
The German Classics of the Nineteenth and Twentieth Centuries........	213
German Confederation, 1815-1866. Bundesversammlung. Protkolle der Detuschen Bundesversammlung, 1816-1866.............................	214
German Drama on Microcards, v.p., 1700-19............................	215
German Foreign Ministry Archives, 1867-1920..........................	216 -218
Germany. Auswartiges Amt. German Foreign Ministry Archives..........	216 -218
Germany, Auswartiges Amt. Politisches Archiv........................	219
Germany. Reichstag. Verhandlungen des Reichstags, 1867-79...........	220
Germany (Allied Occupation, 1945-1949). International Military Tribunal. Trial of the Major War Criminals Before the International Military Tribunal Nuernberg 14 Nov. 1945-1 Oct.1946.....	221
Germany (Allied Occupation 1945-1949). International Military Tribunal. Trials of War Criminals Before the Nurenberg Military Tribunals Under Control Council Law no.10........................	222
The Gerristsen Collection of Women's History, 1543-1945..............	223
Gloucester Cathedral. Mediaeval Registers of St. Peter's Abbey, Gloucester, With Abbot Frocester's History of the Abbey...........	224
Goldsmiths' - Kress Library of Economic Literature: Resources in the Economic, Social, Business and Political History of Modern Industrial Society..	225
Goldwin Smith Papers at Cornell University 1844-1915.................	509
Goss, Charles W.F. The London Directories 1677 to 1855: A Bibliography With Notes on Their Origin and Development...........	371
Gosudarstrennaîa Duma..	482
Graf, Oskar Maria. Nachlass. Papers, 1933-67: Correspondence, MSS. of Novels, Poems, Short Stories, Essays and Speeches..............	226
Great Britain. Bulletins and Other State Intelligence...............	227
Great Britain. Royal Commission Reports Relating to Trade and Labour..	228
Great Britain. Board of Customs and Excise. Ledgers of Exports of Foreign and Colonial Merchandise Under Countries, 1808-1899......	229
Great Britain. Board of Customs and Excise. Ledgers of Imports and Exports, States of Navigation, Commerce and Revenue, 1772-1808...	230
Great Britain. Board of Customs and Excise, Ledgers of Imports Under Countries, 1792-1899..	231
Great Britain. Board of Trade. Census of Production, 1907-1967......	232
Great Britain. Cabinet Office. Cabinet Reports From Prime Ministers to the Crown 1868-1916..	233
Great Britain. Cabinet Office. Photographic Copies of Cabinet Papers, 1880-1916...	234
Great Britain. Central Statistical Office. Annual Abstract of Statistics. v.1-83, 1840-1938.....................................	235
Great Britain. Colonial Office. America and West Indies, Original Correspondence etc., 1606-1808....................................	236
Great Britain. Colonial Office. Annual Report on the Colonies, 1889-1939...	237

	Item No.
Great Britain. Colonial Office. Original Correspondence (With Canada). v.1- 1763-	238
Great Britain. Exchequer. Memoranda Rolls of the Exchequer, 1218-1307	239
Great Britain. Exchequer and Audit Dept. American Loyalist Claims, Series 1, 1776-1831	240
Great Britain. Exchequer and Audit Dept. American Loyalist Claims, Series 2, 1776-1831	241
Great Britain. Foreign and Commonwealth Office. Colonial numbered Series, 1924-60	242
Great Britain Foreign and Commonwealth Office. Colonial Research Publications	243
Great Britain. Foreign Office. British and Foreign State Papers 1812/14-1939	244
Great Britain. Foreign Office. Confidential Prints on China, 1848-1937	246
Great Britain. Foreign Office. Confidential Prints on China and the Far East, 1857-1915	247
Great Britain. Foreign Office. Confidential Prints on Miscellaneous Colonial Conference, North America, American Civil War. South Africa Up to 1916	245
Great Britain. Foreign Office. Correspondence With Her Majesty's Envoy Extraordinary Minister Plenipotentiary in Japan, August 1859-1910	248
Great Britain. Foreign Office. Foreign Office Confidential Papers Relating to China and Her Neighbouring Countries, 1840-1914, With an Additional List 1915-1937	247
Great Britain. Foreign Office. Foreign Office Records FO 800	249
Great Britain. Foreign Office. Foreign Office Registers. n.p., 1822-90	250
Great Britain. Foreign Office. General Correspondence Before 1906. Archives of Conferences, 1813-1822	251
Great Britain. Foreign Office. General Correspondence Before 1906, China 1815-1850	252
Great Britain. Foreign Office. General Correspondence Before 1906, Continent Conferences, 1814-1822	253
Great Britain. Foreign Office. General Correspondence Before 1906, Slave Trade, 1816-1892	254
Great Britain. Foreign Office. General Correspondence Before 1906, United States of America. Series 1, 1782-1795	255
Great Britain. Historical Manuscripts Commission. Guide to the Reports of the Royal Commission on Historical Manuscripts	256
Great Britain. Historical Manuscripts Commission, Publications of the Royal Commission on Historical Manuscripts, Revised to 31st August 1961	256
Great Britain. Historical Manuscripts Commission. Reports. Series 1-81	256
Great Britain. Home Dept. Correspondance H.A. 100/25-27	257
Great Britain. Home Office. Correspondence and Papers, Disturbances 1812-1855	258

                                                                    Item No.

Great Britain. Laws, Statutes, etc. Statutes of the Realm
  (1225-1713).. 259
Great Britain. Ministry of Munitions. History of the Ministry of
  Munitions.. 260
Great Britain. Parliament. The Parliamentary Debates................... 261,263
Great Britain. Parliament. House of Commons. British Sessional
  Papers... 264
Great Britain. Parliament. House of Commons. British Sessional
  Papers. Collection of Indexes, 1696-1900............................... 266
Great Britain. Parliament. House of Commons. Hansard's Catalogue
  and Breviate of Parliamentary Papers, 1696-1834........................ 264
Great Britain. Parliament. House of Commons. General Index to the
  Bills, Reports and Papers Printed by Order of the House of
  Commons and to the Reports and Papers Presented by Command,
  1900-1948-49... 266
Great Britain. Parliament. House of Commons. General Index to the
  Reports From Committees of the House of Commons 1715-1801.............. 268
Great Britain. Parliament. House of Commons. Journals 1547-1900........ 267
Great Britain. Parliament. House of Commons. List of House of
  Commons Sessional Papers, 1701-1750.................................... 264
Great Britain. Parliament. House of Commons. Reports From Committees
  of the House of Commons 1715-1801...................................... 268
Great Britain. Parliament. House of Commons. Sessional Papers of the
  Eighteenth Century 1761-1800... 264
Great Britain. Parliament. House of Lords. A General Index to the
  Sessional Papers Printed by Order of the House of Lords or
  Presented by Special Command....(1801-59).............................. 269
Great Britain. Parliament. House of Lords. Sessional Papers.
  1806-1859.. 269
Great Britain. Privy Council. Acts of the Privy Council of England,
  v.1-43; 1542-1628.. 270
Great Britain. Privy Council. Acts of the Privy Council of England,
  Colonial Series, 1613-1783... 271
Great Britain. Privy Council. Registers, 1631-37....................... 272
Great Britain. Public Record Office. Calendar of Letters and State
  Papers Foreign and Domestic. Henry VIII, 1509-1545..................... 273
Great Britain. Public Record Office. Calendar of State Papers.......... 274
Great Britain. Public Record Office. Calendar of State Papers,
  Colonial Series, 1574-1733... 275
Great Britain. Public Record Office. Calendar of State Papers,
  Domestic Series, Charles I. 1625-1649.................................. 276
Great Britain. Public Record Office. Calendar of State Papers,
  Domestic Series, Charles II, 1660-1670................................. 277
Great Britain. Public Record Offoce. Calendar of State Papers,
  Domestic Series. The Commonwealth, 1649-1660........................... 278
Great Britain. Public Record Office. Calendar of State Papers,
  Domestic Series. Edward VI, Mary, Elizabeth I, James I,
  1547-1625.. 279
Great Britain. Public Record Office. Calendar of State Papers,
  Domestic Series. William III, 1689-95.................................. 280

	Item No.
Great Britain. Public Record Office. Calendar of State Papers, Foreign Series. Edward VI, 1547-1553; Mary, 1553-1558; Elizabeth I, 1558-1582	281
Great Britain. Public Record Office. Foreign Office Records and Consular reports From the Ottoman Empire	282
Great Britain. Public Record Office. F.O. Registers: China, 1865-1915, Coolie Emigration	283
Great Britain. Public Record Office. Guide to the Contents of the Public Record Office	274
Great Britain. Public Record Office. MSS.Calendars and indexes to the Patent Rolls, 1 Elizabeth I - 7 William IV	284
Great Britain. Public Record Office. Rerum Britannicarum Medii Revi Scriptores	285
Great Britain. Public Record Office. Royal Air Force: Final Reports on Operation, - Night Raids	286
Great Britain. Public Record Office. Treasury Minute Books, 1719-22 and 1725-28	287
Great Britain. Public Record office. Unpublished State Papers of English Civil War and Interregnum	288'
Great Britain. Registrar General. Statistical Review of England and Wales. 45v., 1921-65	289
Great Britain. Treasury Solicitor The 1745 Rebellion Papers, 1745-1753	290
Grimes, Louis Arthur. The Collection of the Honourable Louis Arthur Grimes, 1883-1948	291
A Guide to British Foreign Office: Confidential Print: China, 1848-1922. New York, 1970	246
Guide to Japanese Monographs and Japanese Studies of Manchuria, 1945-1960	331
A Guide to Manuscripts Relating to America in Great Britain and Ireland	49
Guide to the Collection of Hungarian Political and Military Records, 1909-45	594
Guide to the Contents of the Public Record Office	274
Guide to the Microfilm Edition of Herstory. Women's History Research Center, 1972	303
Guide to the Microfilm Edition of the Peter B. Porter Papers in the Buffalo and Erie County Historical Society	445
Guide to the Microfilm Edition of the Timothy Pickering Papers	536
Guide in the Microfilm Edition of the Women and Health Collection	630
Guide to the Records of the Moravian Mission Among the Indians of North America	402
A Guide to the Use of United Nations Documents (Including Reference to the Specialized Agencies and Special U.N. Bodies)	545
Gul'binskii, Ignatii Vladislavovich. Literatura Velikogo Desiatiletiia 1917-1927	292
HRAF Source Bibliography	313
Hague. Gemeentemuseum. Muziekbibliotheek. Collection Music Department Haags Gemeentemuseum	293

	Item No.
Haïti. (Republic) Le Moniteur, Journal Officiel de la République d'Haïti..	294
Hakluyt, Richard. The Principal Navigations, Voyages, Traffiques, and Discoveries of the English Nation............................	295
Hakluyt Society. Extra Series, v.1-12...................................	296
Hardy, Thomas. Jude the Obscure; Original MS. From Fitzwilliam Museum, Cambridge...	297
Hardy, Thomas. The Original Manuscripts and Papers of Thomas Hardy..	298
The Harleian Miscellany: or a Collection of Scarce, Curious and Entertaining Pamphlets and Tracts, as Well in Manuscript, as in Print, Found in the Late Earl of Oxford's Library 1808-11.....	299
Harold Jantz Collection...	210
Health, Physical Education and Recreation Microforms Publication Bulletin..	609
Hebrew University Oral History Collection...............................	408
Henderson, George Fletcher. Federal Royal Commission in Canada 1867-1966: A Checklist...	90
Henry Bradshaw Society, London. Publications............................	300
Henry Knox Papers, 1719-1825..	301
Herodotus. Historiae...	302
Herrick, Marvin Theodore. Italian Plays 1500-1700 in the University of Illinois Library..	328
Herstory. Selected Periodicals and Newspapers at the Women's History Research Center Library, Berkeley, Calif........................	303
Herstory Microfilm Collection: Table of Contents........................	303
Hillquit, Morris, 1869-1933. The Morris Hillquit Papers................	304
Hispanic Culture Series...	305
Hispanic Society of America, Library. List of Books Printed Before 1601 in the Library of the Hispanic Society of America...........	305
Histoire Generale des Traites de Paix et Autres Transactions Principales Entre Toutes les Puissances de l'Europe Depuis la Paix de Westphalie...	206
Historical Accounting Literature: A Catalogue of the Collection of Early Works on Bookkeeping and Accounting in the Library of the Institute of Chartered Accountants in England and Wales..........	323
Historical Military Records of the British Army in the American Revolution, 1747-1783..	100
Historical Tracts, a Gift of Mrs. Peter Redpath to the Redpath Library..	306
Historisch - Kritische Beytraege..	382
A History of English Drama, 1660-1900...................................	173
A History of the American Drama From the Beginning to the Civil War....	173
History of the Ministry of Munitions....................................	260
The History of Women. A Comprehensive Collection Based on the holdings of Nine Major Libraries.................................	307
The Hobhouse Letters, 1722-1755...	326
Holyoake Papers, 1831-1905..	308-309
How to Use ERIC...	585

	Item No.
Howell, George. Selected Items From the George Howell Collection at the Bishopsgate Institute, London..	310
Huang Ming Wen Hai...	342
Huegel, Friedrich, Freiherr Von. Diaries, 1877-1924....................	311
The Human Environment Microlibrary...	312
Human Relations Area Files...	313
Human Relations Area Files, Inc. Bibliography of Sources processed for the Files...	313
Human Relations Area Files Inc. HRAF Source Bibliography..............	313
Human Relations Area Files, Inc. Outline of Cultural Materials........	313
Hungarian Peace Negotiations...	314
Hungary. Ministry of Foreign Affairs. Hungarian Peace Negotiations...	314
Imperial Gazetteers of India. India Gazetteers; District (Series) v.1-122..	316
Imperial Gazetteers of India. India Gazetteers; Provincial (Series)..	315
Index to American Federal Censuses, 1790-1890...............................	552
Index to Patrologiae Cursus Completus... Series Graeca..................	397
Index to the Andrew Jackson Papers. U.S. Government Printing Office, 1967...	592
Index to the Chester A. Arthur Papers. U.S. Government Printing Office, 1961...	592
Index to the Franklin Pierce Papers...	592
Index to the Henry Knox Papers Owned by the New England Historic Geneological Society and Deposited in the Massachusetts Historical Society...	301
Index to the James Monroe Papers..	592
Index to the John Tyler Papers...	592
Index to the Records of the United States Exploring Expedition Under the Command of Lieutenant Charles Wilkes, 1839-1842..........	599
Index to the William Henry Harrison Papers...................................	592
Index to the Zachary Taylor Papers...	592
India. Legislature. Legislative Council. Abstracts of the Proceedings of the Council of the Governor-General of India Assembled for the Purpose of Making Laws and Regulations..............................	317
India. Legislature. Legislative Council. Proceedings of the Legislative Council of India Calcutta, 1856-	318
India. Linguistic Survey. Linguistic Survey of India. Calcutta.	319
India Census, 1872-1951. A Checklist and Index...............................	320
India Census, Commissioner. Census of India 1871/72-1951.................	320
Informatech France-Quebec. Bulletin Référence 83...........................	321
Institut Canadien du Film/Canadian Film Institute. Documentation Filmographique/Film Title Index..	322
The Institute of Chartered Accountants: Microfilmed Collection of Rare Books on Accounting and Related Subjects: Complete List of Titles and Index to Contents by Reel.......................................	323
Institute of Chartered Accountants in England and Wales. London. Microfilmed Collection of Rare Books on Accounting and Related Subjects, 15th-19th Centuries...	323
International Developments. A Bibliography...................................	589

	Item No.
International Population Census Publication	324, 325
Isaac Hobhouse and Co. The Hobhouse Letters, 1722-1755; Letters and Other Papers of Isaac Hobhouse and Co	326
Italian Books Before 1601	327
Italian Drama on Microfilm	328
Italian Plays 1500-1700	328
Italy. Foreign Office. The Sonnino Papers	329
JPRS Publications	589
Jamaica. Assembly. Journals, 1663-1826	330
Japanese Monographs	331
Japanese Relocation Camp and Assembly Center Newspapers	332
Jayakar, Mukund Ramrao. Jayakar Papers	333
Jefferson, Thomas. The Writings of Thomas Jefferson With a Comprehensive Analytical Index	334
Jeffersonian Americana From the University of Virginia Library	335
Jennings, Laura. Catalogue of Petrarch Collection in Cornell University Library	130
The Jesuit Relations and Allied Documents; Travels and Explorations of the Jesuit Missionaries in New France, 1610-1791	336
Johann Adolph Scheibens, Critischer Musikus	499
The John L. Lewis Papers, 1879-1969	365
Jones, Hilda V. Catalogue of Parliamentary Papers, 1801-1900, With a Few of Earlier Date	265
Journal of Education for Upper Canada, 1848-1867	87
Journal Officiel de la Republique d'Haiti	294
Journal Officiel de la Republique Francaise. Mar. 1871 - Dec. 1880	193
Journal Officiel de la Republique Francaise Sous la Commune 1871, Paris	194
Journaux de la Chambre d'assemblée Nationale du Bas-Canada, 1792-1837	460
Journaux du Conseil Législatif du Quebec 1867-1968	462
Journaux du Conseil Spécial de la Province du Bas-Canada, 1838-1841	463
Journaux, Période de la Commune	337
K'ang Jih Chan-Cheng Tzu-liao (1)	338
Kentucky Culture	339
Kentucky Microcard Series	340
King, William Lyon Mackenzie. Mackenzie King Diaries, 1893-1931	341
Ku, Ssu-li (comp.) Huang Ming Wen Hai	342
Laborde, Jean Benjamin de. Essai Sur la Musique Ancienne et moderne	343
Labour Party (Great Britain). Report of the Annual Conference 1901-1973	344
Labour Party (Great Britain). Executive Committee. National Executive Committee Minutes of the British Labour Party, 1900-1951	345
Labour Research Department. London. Books and Pamphlets, 1916-72 and continuation	346

                                                                    Item No.

Labour Union Constitutions and Proceedings, 1836-1974................ 347
Lafontaine, Sir Louis Hippolyte. Collection Lafontaine............... 348
Lambeth Palace Library. The Fulham Papers............................ 349
Lambeth Palace Library. Registers of the Archbishops of Canterbury,
    13-17th Centuries.. 350
Landmarks of Science; a Comprehensive Collection of the Source
    Materials in the History of Science.............................. 351
Lands Surveys Branch Record of Initial Land Surveys of Ontario....... 420
Later American Plays 1831-1900: Being a Compilation of the Titles of
    Plays by American Authors Published and Performed in America
    since 1831-1900.. 173
Latin American Documents... 352
Laurendeau, André. Collection d'articles de M. André Laurendeau
    Parus dans Le Devoir, 1947-1967.................................. 353
Laurier, Sir Wilfrid. The Laurier Papers. Series A, B,C,D............ 354
Laurin, Christiana. Les Bio-Bibliographies et Bibliographies
    Compilees par les Etudiants de l'Ecole des Bibliothecaires de
    l'Universite de Montreal: Liste et Index......................... 405
League of Nations. Armaments Yearbook. Category IX. 1924-1940........ 355
League of Nations. Assembly Documents, 1919-1946..................... 356
League of Nations. Circular Letters From the Secretary-General,
    1919-1946.. 357
League of Nations. Council Documents, 1919-1946...................... 358
League of Nations. Documents and Publications, 1919-1946............. 359
League of Nations. Mandate Reports................................... 360
League of Nations. Official Journal. (Records of the Assembly, and
    the Minutes of the Council)...................................... 361
League of Nations. Review of World Trade 1910-1936................... 362
League of Nations. Treaty Series..................................... 363
Ledgers of Exports of Foreign and Colonial Merchandiese Under
    Countries, 1808-1899. (Customs 10)............................... 229
Ledgers of Imports and Exports, States of Navigation, Commerce and
    Revenue, 1772-1808 (Customs 17 nos.1-30)......................... 230
Ledgers of Imports Under Countries, 1792 - 1899. (Customs 4)......... 231
The Left in Britain.. 364
Legal and Miscellaneous Papers. Odessa, 1807-77...................... 415
Lester B. Pearson 1897-1972..
Letters Received by the Secretary of the Navy: Captain's Letters,
    1805-1886..
Letters Received by the Secretary of the Navy From Commanders
    1804-1886.. 596
Letters Received by the Secretary of the Navy From Officers Below the
    Rank of Commander, 1802-1884..................................... 597
Letters Received by the Secretary of War: Registered Series, 1801-
    1806... 605
Letters Received by the Secretary of War: Unregistered Series,
    1789-1860.. 606
Letters Sent by the Secretary of the Navy to Officers, 1798-1868..... 598

	Item No.
Letters Sent by the Secretary of War, Relating to Military Affairs, 1800-1861.	607
Lettres, Instruction Set Memoires de Colbert.	122
Lewis, John Llewellyn, 1880-1969. The John L. Lewis Papers 1879-1969.	365
Library of Church Unity Periodicals. Ser.1-3.	147
Library Science Research Studies. No.1.	366
Lincoln Record Society. Publications.	367
Linguistic Survey of India.	319
List of books printed before 1601 in the Library of the Hispanic Society of America.	305
List of House of Commons Sessional Papers.	264
Literatura Velikogo Desiatiletiia 1917-1927.	292
Literature of Theology and Church History.	368
Liverpool Papers.	369
Log and Journal of Captain Cook's Voyage Round the World in the Bark "Endeavour" 1768-1771.	129
London. Stationer's Company. Records.	370
London Directories From the Guildhall Library, 1677-1900.	371
The London Directories 1677 to 1855: A Bibliography With Notes on Their Origin and Development.	371
The London Theatre; a Collection of the Most Celebrated Dramatic Pieces.	150
London Trades Council. Minutes and Papers, 1860-1953.	372
Losely Manuscripts: Manuscripts of the Revels Office in the Time of Henry VIII, Edward VI and Mary, ca. 1540-1580.	373
The Luddite Papers, 1812-1813.	464
McGill University, Montreal. Library. Catalogue of a Collection of Historical Tracts, 1561-1800.	306
Mackenzie King Diaries 1893-1931. Toronto, University of Toronto Press, 1973.	341
Mackenzie Valley Pipeline Inquiry. Briefs and Transcripts of Public Hearings.	374
Mackenzie Valley Pipeline Inquiry. Index to Briefs and Transcripts.	374
Maclean Hunter Microfilm Services. Lester B. Pearson 1897-1972. Toronto: Maclean Hunter Microfilm Services, 1972. 11 sheets.	375
MacLeod, Roy M. and James R. Friday. Archives of British Men of Science: A Survey of Private and Institutional Holdings of British Scientific Archives.	376
McMahon, A Michael and Stephanie A. Morris. Technology in Industrial America: The Committee on Science and the Arts of the Franklin Institute, 1824-1900.	200
Les Maîtres Musiciens de la Renaissance Français, Editions Publiées par n. Henry Expert.	377
Manitoba. Manitoba Gazette. 1870-.	378
Manitoba. Laws, Statutes, etc. Manitoba Statutes.	379
Manitoba. Laws, Statutes, etc. Revised Statutes, 1891-1902.	379
Manitoba. Legislative Assembly. Journals. 1870-1900.	380
Manitoba. Legislative Council. Journal. 1871-76.	381

	Item No.
Manitoba Gazette. 1870.	378
Manitoba Statutes.	379
Manross, William Wilson. The Fulham Papers in Lambeth Palace Library; American Colonial Section Calendar and Indexes	349
MSS. Calendars and Indexes to the Patent Rolls, 1 Elizabeth I - 7 William IV.n.p., 1558-1837. 15 reels	284
Manuscripts From the Collection in Northampton Central Library	120
Manuscripts of the Revels Office in the Time of Henry VIII, Edward VI and Mary, Ca. 1540-1580	373
Manuscripts of the Works of Charles Dickens From the Forster Collection in the Victoria and Albert Museum, London	152
MSS Records for Natal (Maritzburg) c.1853-1900	548
Marpurg, Friedrich Wilhelm. Historisch - Kritische Beytraege	382
Martens, George F. von, ed. Nouveau Recueil de Traites D'Alliance, de Paix, de Treve, 1817-41	383
Martens, George F. von, ed. Nouveau Recueil Général de Traites, Conventions et Autres Transactions Remarquables, 1843-75	384
Martens, George F. von, ed. Nouveau Recueil Général de Traites et Autres Actes Relatifs aux Rapports de Droit International	385
Martens, George F. von, ed. Nouveau Supplémens du Recueil de Traites	386
Martens, George F. von, ed. Recueil de Traites D'Alliance, de Paix de Trĕve, 1817-1835	387
Martens, George F. von, ed. Supplément au Recueil des Principaux Traites D'Alliance de Paix, de Treve, 1802-1808	388
Martens, George F. von, ed. Table Général du Recueil des Traites, 1875-1876	389
Massachusetts Local Tax List Through 1776	390
Materialien zur Kunde des Aelteren Englischen Dramas	391
Mather, Cotton, The Mather Papers	392
Matsumoto, Tadao. Matsumoto Bunko. Matsumoto Collection of the Press Cuttings Relating to China, the Early Twentieth Century	393
Mediaeval Registers of St. Peter's Abbey, Gloucester, With Abbot Frocester's History of the Abbey	224
Memoranda Rolls of the Exchequer, 1218-1307	239
Menshevik Collection of Newspapers, Periodicals, Pamphlets and Books Related to the Menshevik Movement	394
The Messages Between Franklin D. Roosevelt and Winston Churchill, 1939-1945, and Related Materials.	476
Metropolitan Toronto Central Library. Biographical Scrapbooks	395
A Microform Library. Sources for the History of Social Welfare in America	396
Microfilmed Collection of Rare Books and Accounting Related Subjects, 15th-19th Centuries	323
Migne, Jaques Paul. Patrologiae Cursus Completus : Series Graeca. Paris, 1857-87	397
Migne, Jaques Paul. Patrologiae Cursus Completus : Series Latina. Paris, 1844-1882	398

	Item No.
Missionary Periodicals From the China Mainland.............................	399
Monthly Catalogue of United States Government Publications.............	533,604
Montreal, Université de. École de Bibliothécaires. Bibliographies D'Auteurs Canadiens D'Expression Française...........................	400
Monuments Germaniao Historica Inde ab anno Christi Quingentesimo Usque ad Annum Millesimum et Quingentesimum.......................	401
Monuments Historiques Relatifs aux Règnes d'Alexis Michaelowitch, Feodor III, et Pierre le Grand, Czars de Russie, Extraits des Archives du Vatican et de Naples....................................	532
Moore, John Robert. A Checklist of the Writings of Daniel Defoe......	146
Moravian Church of the American Indian Mission. Missionary Records of Moravian Church of the American Indian Mission.................	402
The Morris Hillquit Papers...	304
Moscow, Publicahnaîa Biblioteka. Eighteenth Century Russian Publications...	403
Murdock, George P. Ethnographic Atlas.................................	313
Murdock, George P. Outline of World Cultures, 2nd ed. rev............	313
Musicache...	404
Nachlass. Papers, 1933-67: Correspondence, MSS. of Novels, Poems, Short Stories, Essays and Speeches, Many of Which are Unpublished, Photos, Clippings and Memorabilia.......................	226
National Executive Committee Minutes of the British Labour Party, 1900-1951...	345
National Film Archive, London. Film Title Index......................	405
Nationalsozialistische Deutsche Arbeiter Partei. Hauptarchiv. NSDAP Hauptarchiv (Nazi Party Archives)..........................	406
The Negro in America: Research Memoranda for Use in the Preparation of Dr. Gunnar Myrdal's An American Dilemma. 1940..................	102
New Hebrides Manuscripts on Microform.................................	407
New York Public Library. French Revolutionary Pamphlets; a Checklist of the Talleyrand and Other Collections.....................	203
New York Public Library. Rare Book Division. Checklist of Additions to Evans' American Bibliography in the Rare Book Division........	162
New York Times Oral History Program...................................	408
Newberry Library, Chicago. A Checklist of Courtesy Books in the Newberry Library...	409
Newberry Library, Chicago. Courtesy Books, 1571-1773. (From Collections in the Newberry Library)..............................	409
Newberry Library, Chicago. French Political Pamphlets, 1560-1654, From Collections in Newberry Library...............................	410
Newfoundland. Legislative Assembly. Journals, 1866-1900 (b) Statutes, 1866-1891...	411
Newspapers on Microfilm. A Catalogue..................................	93
Nichols, John Gough. A Descriptive Catalogue of the First Series of the Works of the Camden Society 1806-1873.........................	57
Nicoll, Allardyce. A History of English Drama 1660-1900..............	173
Nineteenth Century American Literature and History. See American Literature of the 19th Century.....................................	14

	Item No.

Northern Ireland Political Literature., Phase I, 1968-72, Phase II, 1973-75. Collection in the Lindenhall Library, Belfast.......... 412
Notes From the British Legation in the United States to the Department of State, 1791-1906................................... 575
Notes From the Department of State to Foreign Ministers and Consuls in the U.S. 1793-1834.. 576
Notes to Foreign Legations in United States From the Department of State. Great Britain, 1834-1906..................................... 577
Nottinghamshire Parish Registers: Marriages, 1898-1915............... 413
Obscestvennoe Dvizenie v. Rossii v Nachnale XX-veka................... 414
Odessa Miscellanea. Legal and Miscellaneous Papers. Odessa, 1807-77... 415
O'Donovan Rossa, Jeremiah. O'Donovan Rossa Papers.................... 416
Office des Comminications Sociales, Montreal. Documentation Filmographique... 417
Ontario. Chief Election Officer. Return From the Records of the Legislative Assembly of the Province of Ontario. 1867-1975....... 418
Ontario. Dept. of Crown Lands. Reports and Field Notes of Surveyors no.1-867. (Includes Township Plans)............................. 419
Ontario. Dept. of Lands and Forests. Lands Surveys Branch, Record of Initial Land Surveys of Ontario............................. 420
Ontario. Laws, Statutes, etc. Statutes of the Province of Ontario.... 421
Ontario. Legislative Assembly. Debates 1867-1953..................... 422
Ontario. Legislative Assembly. Journal. v.1-, 1867................... 423
Ontario. Legislative Assembly. Sessional Papers. v.1-80, 1867/68-1968... 424
Organization of American States. Actas de las Sessiones, 1946-1961.. 425
Organization of American States. Documentos Officiales/Official Documents.. 426
Organization of American States. Minutes of Meetings, 1948-1960..... 427
The Original Manuscripts and Papers of Thomas Hardy.................. 298
Orlando; MS From Knole Kent.. 631
Outline of Cultural Materials.. 313
Owen, Robert. Robert Owen Papers 1821-58............................ 428
Palais de Justice de Montreal. Archives. Recensement 1741 de la Compagnie des Indes.. 429
Pamiatniki Diplomaticheskikh Snoshenii Drevnei Rossii s Derzhavami Inostrannymi. 1851-1871.. 430
Pamphlets in the Public Archives, 1493-1877.......................... 74
Pamphlets of Socialism, Communism, Bolshevism, etc., 1849-1931....... 431
Panama Canal Studies, 1946-48.. 582
The Papers of Albert Gallatin.. 205
Papers of Francis Place, (1771-1854) Illustrative of the Reform Crisis 1830-2.. 443
The Papers of William Penn... 432
Papers Relating to the Foreign Relations of the United States, 1861-1942... 578
Papyrology on Microfiche. Ser.1...................................... 435

	Item No.
Paris. Peace Conference, 1919. Select Reports of the American Commission to Negotiate the Peace....................................	434
Parker Society. Publications, v.1-55. 1849-1855.....................	435
Partai Komunis Indonesia. Publications of the Communist Party of Indonesia, Djakarta, Pembarvan, 1945-1964..........................	436
Patrologiae Cursus Completus: Series Graeca. Paris...................	397
Pearson, John Batteridge. A Complete List of the Names of the Authors Whose Works are Printed in the Greek Series of Migne's Patrologia...	398
Pearson, John Batteridge. Conspectus Auctorum Quorum Nomina Indicibus Patrologiae Graeco-Latinae a J.P. Migne Editae Continentur...	398
Peel, Bruce Braden. A Bibliography of the Prairie Provinces to 1953 With Biographical Index...	437
Peel Bibliography on Microfiche.......................................	437
Peirce, Charles Santiago Sanders. The Charles S. Peirce Papers, Cambridge...	438
Peirce, Charles Santiago Sanders. Complete Works.....................	439
Penn, Thomas. The Thomas Penn Papers, 1729-1832, at the Historical Society of Pennsylvania...	440
Penn, William. The Papers of Will Penn. See The Papers of William Penn..	432
Pennsylvania. University Library. The Maclure Collection of French Revolutionary Materials...	202
Pervaĭa Vseobshchaĭa Perepis' Naseleniĭa Rossiĭskoĭ Imperial 1897......	485
Peter B. Porter Papers..	445
Petites Revues d'avant-garde, Dadaistes, Surréalistes, ou Apparentées, 1912-1933...	441
Petrarch Collection...	130
Phonefiche..	
Place, Francis. Papers of Francis Place (1771-1854) Illustrative of the Reform Crisis 1830-2..	443
The Plains and the Rockies..	444
Poems in Letters to Walter London by Robert Southey...................	519
Politics and Administration of Tudor England..........................	52
Pollard, A.W. A Short-title Catalogue of Books Printed in England, Scotland and Ireland and of English Books Printed Abroad 1475-1640..	174, 176
Polnoe Sobranie Zakonov Russiĭskoĭ Imperii 1649-1916...................	483
Porter, Peter Buel. Peter B. Porter Papers (and Those of His Grandson, Peter A. Porter (1853-1925) in the Buffalo and Erie County Historical Society.....................................	445
Praetorius, Michael. Syntagma Musicum ex Veterum et Recentiorum, Ecclesiasticorum Autorum Lectione, 1615-1620.......................	446
The Press Conference of Franklin D. Roosevelt, 1933-1945..............	477
Prince Edward Island. Laws, Statutes, etc. Statutes, 1867-1900.......	447
Prince Edward Island. Legislative Assembly. Journals, 1788-..........	448
Prince Edward Island. Legislative Council. Debates and Proceedings. 1867-93...	449

Item No.

Prince Edward Island. Legislative Council. Journals 1867-1893.......	450
Prince Society. Publications. Boston, 1865-1920.....................	451
The Principal Navigations, Voyages, Traffiques, and Discoveries of the English Nation..	295
Printed Plays of Lope de Vega and Others............................	620
Privy Council Registers, 1631-37....................................	272
Proceedings of the Legislative Council of India Calcutta, 1856.......	318
Profile; Canadian Provincial and Municipal Publications, 1973........	452
Protkolle der Deutschen Bundesversammlung, 1816-1866................	214
Province in Rebellion: Documentary History of the Founding of the Commonwealth of Massachusetts, 1774-1775..........................	453
Prussia. Landtag. Haus der Abgeordneten. Stenographische Berichte, 1849-1891..	454
Prussia. Landtag. Herrenhaus. Stenographische Berichte, 1849/50-1916/18...	455
Pubester, Henry J. State Censuses: An Annotated Bibliography of Censuses of Population Taken After the Year 1790 by States and Territories of the United States..............................	521
Publicat; A Canadian Federal Documents Service, 1977-...............	456
Publications of the Communist Party of Indonesia, Djakarta, Pembarvan 1945-1964..	436
Quebec. Commission Gendron. Documents de la Commission et Audiences Publiques..	457
Quebec. Ministère de l'Éducation. Office de la Langue Française. Centre de Terminologie. Fiches de Terminologie...................	458
Quebec (Province). Assemblée Nationale. Documents de la Session, 1867-1972..	459
Quebec (Province). Législature. Assemblée Legislatif. Journaux de la Chambre d'assemblée Nationale du Bas-Canada, 1792-1837.........	460
Quebec (Province). Législature. Conseil Législatif. Journaux du Conseil Législatif de la Provice du Bas-Canada, 1792-1837........	461
Quebec (Province). Législature. Conseil Legislatif. Journaux du Conseil Legislatif du Quebec 1867-1968............................	462
Quebec (Province). Législature. Conseil Spécial. Journaux du Conseil Spécial de la Province du Bas-Canada, 1838-1841..........	463
Quebec Literary and Historical Society Documents (1838-1915).........	91
Quinn, Arthur Hobson. A History of the American Drama From the Beginning to the Civil War.......................................	173
Quinn, Arthur Hobson. A History of the American Drama From the Civil War to the Present Day.....................................	173
Radcliffe, Sir Joseph. The Luddite Papers, 1812-1813................	464
Radical Periodicals in the United States; 1890-1960.................	465
Radical Periodicals of Great Britain, 1794-1950.....................	466
Rare Militant British 19th Century Freethought Books................	467
Recensement 1741 de la Compagnie des Indes..........................	429
Die Recesse und Andere Akten der Hansetage von 1256-1430............	468
Recessions, Depressions, and Economic Panics in American History; Collection of Sources, 1815-1974.................................	469

Item No.

Records of Negotiations Connected With the Treaty of Ghent;
　　Despatches From the American Commissioners, Aug. 29, 1813-
　　July 3, 1815.. 579
Records of the Committee on Science and the Arts of the Franklin
　　Institute, 1824-1900... 200
Records of the Russian-American Company, 1802-1867................. 593
Records of the Secretary of War; Letters Sent to the President,
　　1800-1863.. 608
Records of the U.S. Consulate in Kunming, 1922-28.................. 580
Records of the United States Exploring Expedition Under the
　　Command of Lieutenant Charles Wilkes, 1838-1842................ 599
Recueil des Historiens des Gaules et de la France. 1738-1904....... 470
Registers of the Archbishops of Canterbury, 13-17th Centuries...... 350
Register of Debates in the Congress of the U.S. Second Session of
　　the Eighteenth Congress, Dec.6, 1824. First Session of the
　　Twenty-fifth Congress, Oct.16, 1837............................ 563
Registrar General's Statistical Review of England and Wales 1921-
　　1965... 288
Reguerro, Jose M. Spanish Drama of the Golden Age.................. 511
Religion in America: Dissertations................................. 471
Religion in America: Early Books and Manuscripts................... 472
Reparation Papers of the Allied Powers Reparation Commission, 1920-
　　1930... 9
Repertoire Chronologique et Analytique des arrets du Conseil des
　　depeches 1611-1710... 198
Rerum Britannicarum Medii Revi Scriptores.......................... 285
Resources in the Economic, Social, Business and Political History of
　　Modern Industrial Society...................................... 225
Return From the Records of the Legislative Assembly of the Province
　　of Ontario. 1867-1975.. 418
Review of World Trade 1910-1936.................................... 362
The Revolutionary Diplomatic Correspondence of the U.S. 1889....... 581
Rhoda Kellogg Child Art Collection................................. 473
Richardson, Samuel. Correspondence, 1748-62........................ 474
Robert Owen Papers 1821-58... 428
Robin, Richard S. Annotated Catalogue of the Papers of Charles S.
　　Peirce, by Richard S. Robin.................................... 438
Robin, Richard S. The Peirce Papers, A Supplementary Catalogue..... 438
Roden, Robert F. Later American Plays 1831-1900: Being a Compilation
　　of the Titles of Plays by American Authors Published and
　　Performed in America Since 1831-1900........................... 173
Rohn, Peter H. World Treaty Index.................................. 363
Rolle, Richard, of Hampole. Prick of Conscience.................... 475
Roosevelt, Franklin Delano. The Messages Between Franklin D.
　　Roosevelt and Winston Churchill, 1939-1945, and Related
　　Materials.. 476
Roosevelt, Franklin D. The Press Conference of Franklin D.
　　Roosevelt 1933-1945. 2nd ed.................................... 477

                                                                              Item No.

Le Rousseauisme, 1788-1797.. 478
Royal Alexandra Theatre; (A Collection of Newspaper Clippings With
    Reviews of Stage Performances at This Theatre Toronto, 1911-
    65.. 479
Royal Institute for the Advancement of Learning. "Letter Books"
    1820-1855. Letters. 1820-1849....................................... 480
Russell Papers: Correspondence. v.p., 1863-1865........................ 481
Russia. Gosudarstvennaîa Duma. Gosudarstrennaîa Duma. Extended-
    Micro Edition of International Documentation Centre............... 482
Russia. Laws, Statutes, etc. Polnoe Sobranie Zakonov Rossiĭskoĭ
    Imperii 1649-1916... 483
Russia. Treaties, etc. Recueil des Traites et Conventions Conclus
    par la Russie avec les Puissances Etrangeres...................... 484
Russia. Tsentral'nyĭ statisticheskiĭ Komitet. Pervaîa Vseobshchaîa
    Perepis' Naseleniîa Rossiĭskoĭ Imperii 1897g...................... 485
Russia. Tsentralnyĭ Statisticheskiĭ Komitet. Statistika Rossiĭkoĭ
    Imperii, Petrograd. 1887-1916.. 486
Russia. Voennoe Ministerstvo. Stolîetîe Voennago Ministerstva,
    1802-1902.. 487
Russia (1917-R.S.F.S.R.) Verkhovnyĭ Sovet. Vedomosti.................. 488
Russia (1923-U.S.S.R.) S'ezd Sovetov. Stenograficheskiĭ Otchet,
    1922-35.. 489
Russia (1923-U.S.S.R.) Treaties. etc. Sbornik Deĭstvîuishchick
    Dogorov, Soglashenii i Konventsii, 1928-1967..................... 490
Russia (1923-U.S.S.R.) Verkhovnyĭ Sovet. Vedomosti................... 491
Russia Letters s.l.n.d... 492
Russian Futurism, 1910-1916.. 493
Russian Historical Sources. Series 1 and 2............................ 494
La Russie et l'opinion Francaise au 19e Siècle........................ 495
Russkoe Istoricheskoe Obshchestvo, Leningrad. Sbornik, 1-148;
    1867-1916.. 496
Sabin, Joseph. Bibliotheca Americana: A Dictionary of Books
    Relating to America From its Discovery to the Present Time....... 335
Sacrorum Conciliorum nova et Amplissima Collectis..................... 497
Saricks, Ambrose. A Bibliography of the Frank E. Melvin Collection
    of Pamphlets of the French Revolution in the University of
    Kansas Libraries.. 203
Sbornik Deĭstvîuishchick Dogorov, Soglashenii i Konventsii, 1928-
    1967... 490
Scadding, Henry. The Diaries of Henry Scadding........................ 498
Scheibe, Johann Adolph. Johann Adolph Scheibens, Critischer
    Musikus.. 499
Schein, Johann Hermann. Complete Collected Musical Works............ 500
Schomburg Center for Research in Black Culture. A Selection of
    titles from the Schomberg Center for Research in Black Culture:
    Series 2. 1534-1955.. 501
Scott, Sir Walter Bart. A Collection of Scarce and Valuable
    Tracts on the Most Entertaining subjects. 1809-1815.............. 502

	Item No.
Scottish Text Society, Edinburgh. Publications : no. 1-65. 1884-1918	503
A Second Checklist of French Political Pamphlets 1560-1653, in the Newberry Library	410
A Select Collection of Old English Plays	160
Selected Items From the George Howell Collection at the Bishopsgate Institute	310
Selected Periodicals and Newspapers at the Women's History Research Center Library. Berkeley Calif.	303
A Selection of Titles From the Schomberg Center for Research in Black Culture : Series 2. 1534-1955	501
Selections From China Mainland Magazines. no. 1-Aug.15,1955-	564
Sessional Papers of the Dominion of Canada 1867-1925	67
The 1745 Rebellion Papers, 1745-1753	290
Seventeenth Century English Pamphlets by Various Authors. From the Collection of the New York Public Library	504
The Shaker Collection of the Western Reserve Historical Society	505
Shaw, Ralph R. American Bibliography; A Preliminary Checklist for 1801-1819	163
Shih-sou tzu liao shih kung fei tzu liao	110
Shipton, Clifford Kenyon. National Index of American Imprints through 1800; the Short-title Evans by Clifford Shipton and James E. Mooney	162
A Short-title Catalogue of Books Printed in England, Scotland and Ireland and of English Books Printed abroad 1475-1640, Compiled by A. W. Pollard and G.R. Redgrave	176
Short-title Catalogue of Books Printed in France and of French Books Printed in Other Countries From 1470 to 1600 in the British Museum. London, 1966	201
Short-title Catalogue of Books Printed in Italy and of Books Printed Abroad 1501-1600	327
Short-title Catalogue of Books Printed in Other Countries From 1465-1600 Now in the British Museum	327
Short-title Catalogue of Books Printed in Spain and of Spanish Books Printed Elsewhere in Europe Before 1601 Now in the British Museum, London	305
Short-title Catalogue of Books Printed in the German-speaking Countries...From 1455 to 1600 Now in the British Museum	212
Short-title Catalogue of Books Printed in the Netherlands and Belgium and of Dutch and Flemish Books	31
Simon Diaz, J. Bibliografia de Literatura Hispanica Madrid	305
Skeat, Walter William. Twelve Facsimilies of Old English Manuscripts	506
The Slave Trade and Abolitionism in France and its Colonies, 1744-1848	507
Slavery Source Materials	508
Smith, Goldwin. Goldwin Smith Papers at Cornell University, 1844-1915	509

	Item No.
Social and Economic Development Plans	510
Social Problems and the Churches: The Harlan Paul Douglass Collection of Religious Research Reports	511
Société des Anciens Textes Français, Paris. Publications no.1-70. 1875-1925	512
Society for the Propagation of the Faith. Quebec (Diocese). Rapport sur les missions du Diocese de Quebec. no.1-21, Jan 1839 - Mai 1874	513
Society for the Propagation of the Gospel in Foreign Parts, London	514
Somerset Parish Registers: Marriages, 1898-1915	515
Sotheby, Firm, Auctioneers, London. Catalogue of Sales. 1734-1945	516
Source Materials in the Field of Theatre	517
South Africa; a Collection of Political Documents Covering the Years 1902-1963	518
Southey, Robert. Poems in Letters to Walter London by Robert Southey Plus Additional Letters to W.S. Landor	519
Soviet Union; Bibliography - Index to U.S. JPRS Research Translations	589
Spanish Drama of the Golden Age	511
Stanford University Project South Oral History Collection	408
State Censuses, 1795-1934	521
State Succession Debates	522
Statistical Abstract of the United States, 1878-1955	523
Statistical Review of England and Wales	288
Statistics Canada. Publications, 1841-1975	524
Statistika Rossiĭkoĭ Imperii, Petrograd. 1887-1916	486
Statutes of the Province of Ontario	421
Statutes of the Realm (1225-1713)	259
Stenograficheskiĭ Otchet, 1922-35	489
Stenographische Berichte, 1849/50-1916/18	455
Stevens, Benjamin Franklin, comp. Facsimiles of Manuscripts in European Archives Relating to America, 1773-1783	525
Stoletie Voennago Ministerstva, 1802-1902	487
Strachan, John Papers	526
The Stuart Papers From the Denys Eyre Bower Collection	527
The Stuart Papers From the Royal Archives in Windsor Castle	528
Studi Secenteschi, v.2-7, 9 etc. (Bibliographies Each on a Particular Part of the Collezione Palatina)	190
Studies in the Early English Periodical	177
Subject Index to the U.S. Joint Publications Research Service Translations	589
Supplement to Charles Evans' American Bibliography	162
Survey of China Mainland Press. Nov.1, 1950-. Dec.1957. Hong Kong	565
Svodnyi Katalog Russkoi Knigi Grazhdanskoi Pechati XVIII veka, 1725-1800	171
Syntagma Musicum ex Veterum et Recentiorum, Ecclesiasticorum Autorum Lectione, 1615-1620	446

	Item No.
Tanjur. Cone Tanjur. 209v.	529
Teapot Dome Documents. Edited by John Mascato	530
Technology in Industrial America: the Committee on Science and the Arts of the Franklin Institute, 1824-1900	200
Ten years of United Nations Publications, 1945 to 1955, a Complete Catalogue	547
Le Théatre de la Révolution et de l'Empire: 132 pièces de Théatre Selectionnées et Présentées par Marc Regaldo; Avec le Concours du Centre d'études du XVIII Siècle	531
Theiner, Augustin. Monuments Historiques Relatifs aux Règnes d'Alexis Michaelowitch, Feodor III, et Pierre le Grand, Czars de Russie, Extraits des Archives du Vatican et de Naples	532
The Thomas Penn Papers, 1729-1832, at the Historical Society of Pennsylvania	440
Thomason Tracts, 1640-1661. Films, 1977-	533
Thompson, L.S. A Bibliography of French Plays on Microcards	535
Thompson, Lawrence S. A Bibliography of French Revolutionary Pamphlets on Microfiche	203
Thompson, L.S., A Bibliography of Spanish Plays on Microcards	192
Three Centuries of Drama., (English Drama, 1500-1800 and American Drama, 1741-1830)	534
Three Centuries of English and American Plays, a Checklist. England: 1500-1800; United States: 1714-1830	534
Three Centuries of French Drama. v.p. 1600-1899	535
The Timothy Pickering Papers	536
Toronto. Public Library. A Bibliography of Canadiana (1534-1867) in the Toronto Public Library; Edited by Frances M. Staton and Marie Tremaine	99
Toronto. Stock Exchange. Company Reports	537
Trade Statistics of Asian Countries	6, 7
Trades Union Congress. Parliamentary Committee. Minutes, 1888-1922.	538
Transcript of the Trial in the Case of the Attorney-General of the Government of Israel VS Adolf	170
Transdex: Bibliography and Index to the United States Joint Publications Research Service (JPRS) Translations	589
Transdex: JPRS Documents	539
Travels in the New South, 1865-1955	540
Travels in the Old South, 1527-1860	541
Tremaine, Marie. A Bibliography of Canadian Imprints, 1751-1800	92
Trial of the Major War Criminals Before the International Military Tribunal Nuremberg 14 Nov. 1945- 1 Oct. 1946	221
Trials of War Criminals Before the Nuremberg Military Tribunals Under Control Council Law no.10	222
Tson-Kha-Pa Blo-Bzan-Grags-Pa, 1357-1419. Yab Sras Gsun Bum/Tson Kha Pa (Rje)	542
The Tudor Facsimile Texts. Old English Plays: Printed and manuscript rarities. Edited by John S. Farmer	543
Turkey Letters	544

Item No.

Twelve Facsimilies of Old English Manuscripts; with Transcriptions and an Introduction by the Rev. Walter W. Skeat.......	506
The Underground and Alternative Press in Britain........................	545
United Nations: A Doctoral Dissertation Collection. 1866-............	546
United Nations. Documents and Official Records, 1946-.................	547
United Nations. Dept. of Public Information. Ten Years of United Nations Publications, 1945 to 1955, a Complete Catalogue.........	547
United Society for the Propagation of the Gospel. African Archives of the USPG. London (n.d.) MSS Records for Natal (Maritzburg) c.1853-1900..	548
U.S. Bureau of Indian Affairs. Commissioner. Annual Reports 1824-1949..	549
U.S. Bureau of the Census. Census Publications 1790-1916.............	550
U.S. Bureau of the Census. Decennial Census Publications, 1900-1960..	551
U.S. Bureau of the Census. Federal Population Censuses, 1790-1890....	552
U.S. Bureau of the Census. Seventeenth Decennial Census..............	553
U.S. Bureau of the Census. Sixteenth Decennial Census 1940...........	554
U.S. Bureau of the Census. Statistical Abstracts of the United States. 1878-1955...	555
U.S. Congress. American State Papers, 1789-1838. Serial Set, 15th Congress 1817-...	557
U.S. Congress. (Committee Hearings, Prints), 81st. - 84th. Congress, 1949-56..	558
U.S. Congress. (Committee Hearings, Prints), 85th-87th (2nd session) Congress, 1957-1962..	559
U.S. Congress. Congressional Globe. Twenty-third Congress, Dec.2, 1833-Forty-second Congress, March 3, 1873.............................	560
U.S. Congress. Congressional Record, Forty-third Congress, Dec.1, 1873-..	561
U.S. Congress. The Debates and Proceedings in the Congress of the U.S., First Session, March 3, 1789 - Eighteenth Session, May 27, 1824...	562
U.S. Congress. Register of Debates in the Congress of the U.S. Second Session of the Eighteenth Congress, Dec.6, 1824-first....	563
U.S. Consulate General. Hongkong. Selections From China Mainland Magazines. no.1- Aug. 15, 1955-..	564
U.S. Consulate General. Hongkong. Survey of China Mainland Press. Nov.1, 1950- Dec. 1957...	565
U.S. Consulate General, Hongkong. Agricultural Attache's Office. Agricultural Information on Mainland China, 1953-1967............	566
U.S. Consulate General, Hongkong. Agricultural Attache's Office. Collection of Agricultural Information on Mainland China, 1948-1967...	567
U.S. Dept. of State. Consular Despatches, 1790-1906...................	568
U.S. Dept. of State. Despatches From United States Consuls, Hamilton, Ont. 1867-1906..	569
U.S. Dept. of State. Despatches From United States Ministers to China, 1843-1906..	570

Item No.

U.S. Dept. of State. Despatches From United States Ministers to
Great Britain, 1791-1906.. 571
U.S. Dept. of State. Diplomatic Instructions of the Department of
State, 1801-1906... 572
U.S. Dept. of State. Foreign Relations of the United States.
Diplomatic Papers, 1861-1956... 573
U.S. Dept. of State. Miscellaneous Letters of the Dept. of State.... 574
U.S. Dept. of State. Notes From the British Legation in the United
States to the Department of State, 1791-1906............................. 575
U.S. Dept. of State. Notes From the Department of State to Foreign
Ministers and Consuls in the U.S. 1793-1834.............................. 576
U.S. Dept. of State. Notes to Foreign Legations in United States
From the Department of State. Great Britain, 1834-1906................... 577
U.S. Dept. of State. Papers Relating to the Foreign Relations of the
United States, 1861-1942... 578
U.S. Dept. of State. Records of Negotiations Connected With the
Treaty of Ghent; Despatches From the American Commissioners,
Aug.29, 1813-July 3, 1815.. 579
U.S. Dept. of State. Records of the U.S. Consulate in Kunming,
1922-28.. 580
U.S. Dept. of State. The Revolutionary Diplomatic Correspondence of
the U.S. 1889.. 581
U.S. Dept. of the Army. Caribbean Defense Command. Panama Canal
Studies.. 582
U.S. Dept. of the Treasury. Annual Reports of the Secretary of the
Treasury on the State of Finances 1790-1974.............................. 583
U.S. Educational Resources Information Center. (Papers From ca.18
Clearinghouses on): 1. Adult Education; 2. Disadvantaged;
3. Educational Technology; 4. Rural Education; 5. Reading;
6. Library and Information Science; etc.................................. 584
U.S. Educational Resources Information Center. Catalog of Selected
Documents on the Disadvantaged (ERIC Educational Documents
Index, 1966-1969.)... 584
U.S. Educational Resources Information Center. ERIC Documents........ 585
U.S. Educational Resources Information Center. How to Use ERIC...... 585
U.S. Embassy. France. The U.S. and France: Correspondence Dealing
With Economic Relations, 1811-1930....................................... 586
U.S. Federal Bureau of Investigation. Uniform Crime Reports,
1930-72.. 587
U.S. Foreign Broadcast Information Service. Daily Report............. 588
U.S. Joint Publications Research Service. JPRS Publications.......... 589
U.S. Joint Publications Research Service. Weekly Report on
Communist China Prepared by Foreign Documents Division, Central
Intelligence Agency.. 590
U.S. Library of Congress. Cyrillic Union Catalogue................... 591
U.S. Library of Congress. Manuscript Division. Index to the Andrew
Jackson Papers... 592
U.S. Library of Congress. Manuscript Division. Index to the Chester
A. Arthur Papers... 592

	Item No.
U.S. Library of Congress. Manuscript Division. Index to the Franklin Pierce Papers..	592
U.S. Library of Congress. Manuscript Division. Index to the James Monroe Papers..	592
U.S. Library of Congress. Manuscript Division. Index to the William Henry Harrison Papers..	592
U.S. Library of Congress. Manuscript Division. Presidential Papers..	592
U.S. National Archives. Collection of Hungarian Political and Military Records, 1909-1945..	593
U.S. National Archives. Federal Population Censuses, 1790-1890......	552
U.S. National Archives. Guide to the Collection of Hungarian Political and Military Records, 1909-45................................	593
U.S. National Archives. List of National Archives Microfilm Publications, 1968...	568
U.S. National Archives. Records of the Russian-American Company, 1802-1867...	594
U.S. Navy Dept. Letters Received by the Secretary of the Navy: Captain's Letters, 1805-1886..	595
U.S. Navy Dept. Letters Received by the Secretary of the Navy From Commanders, 1804-1886...	596
U.S. Navy Dept. Letters Received by the Secretary of the Navy From Officers Below the Rank of Commander, 1802-1884.......................	597
U.S. Navy Dept. Letters Sent by the Secretary of the Navy to Officers, 1798-1868..	598
U.S. Navy Dept. Records of the United States Exploring Expedition Under the Command of Lieutenant Charles Wilkes, 1838-1842........	599
U.S. Office of Strategic Services. Intelligence and Research Reports..	600
U.S. President's Commission on the Assissination of President Kennedy. Hearings and Reports, 1964.................................	601
U.S. President's Commission on the Assassination of President Kennedy. (Warren Commission). Hearings..............................	602
U.S. Secretary of State. Press Conferences, 1922-1973...............	603
U.S. Superintendent of Documents. Government Publications. ser.1, 1956- (Depository) ser.2, 1953- (Non Depository).................	604
U.S. Superintendent of Documents. Monthly Catalogue of United States Government Publications. 1895-................................	604
U.S. War Dept. Letters Received by the Secretary of War. Registered Series, 1801-1806...	605
U.S. War Dept. Letters Received by the Secretary of War: Unregistered Series, 1789-1860.......................................	606
U.S. War Dept. Letters Sent by the Secretary of War, Relating to Military Affairs, 1800-1861..	607
U.S. War Dept. Records of the Secretary of War: Letters Sent to the President, 1800-1863..	608
The U.S. and France: Correspondence Dealing With Economic Relations, 1811-1930..	586
University Microfilms, Ann Arbor, Mich. English Books, 1475-1640. A Partial List by STC Numbers. 1938-..................................	174

	Item No.
University Microfilms, Ann Arbor Mich. English Books, 1641-1700; a Partial List of Microfilms by Wing Numbers	175
University of Oregon College of Health, Physical Education and Recreation. Microform Publications	609
Unpublished State Papers of English Civil War and Interregnum	287
Upcott Collection of Literary Autographs, 1765-1830	610
Upper Canada (1791-1840). The Upper Canada Gazette or American Oracle	611
Urban Canada, a Current Index to CanadianPublications in the Field of Urban and Regional Planning and Development. 1977-	612
Urban Documents Microfiche Collection	613
Utopias au siècle des Lumières	614
Van Marum, Martinus. Van Marum Collection: Manuscripts of Essays, Lecture Notes, Diaries	615
Vassall, William. Letter Books, 1769-1800	616
Vatikanishche Quellen zur Geschichte der Papstlichen Hof-und Finanzver-waltung, 1316-1378	617
Vega Carpio, Lope Felix de. Comedias	618
Vega Carpio, Lope Felix de. Copy and Holograph MSS	619
Vega Carpio, Lope Felix de. Printed Plays of Lope de Vega and Others	620
Verhandlungen des Reichstags, 1867-79	220
Verreau. Hospice Anthelme. Fonds Verreau: du carton I au carton IX.	
Victoria and Albert Museum, London. Dept. of Prints and Drawings. Architectural Drawings in the Victoria and Albert Museum	622
Voltaire, Francois Marie Arouet de. Oeuvres Completes nouv. ed	623
Von Chorba, Albert. Checklist of American Drama Published in the English Colonies of North America and the United States Through 1865	173
Wagner, Henry R. The Plains and the Rockies; a Bibliography of Original Narratives of Travel and Adventure, 1800-1865	444
Webster, Daniel. Papers	624
Weekly Report on Communist China, Prepared by Foreign Documents Division, Central Intelligence Agency	590
Wenck, Friedrich August Wilhelm. Codex Juris Gentium Recentissimi, 1781-1795	625
West Indies Mission Records, 1819-1861	117
Westminster Cathedral. Archives. Westminster Cathedral Archives, Series	626
Wing, Donald G. Short Title Catalogue of Books Printed in England... 1641-1700	175
Wisconsin, State Historical Society. Collection of Communist Pamphlets, 1929-1949	627
Wittgenstein, Ludwig. The Wittgenstein Papers	628
Wolfenbuettel. Herzog-August-Bibliothek. Libretti	629
Women and/in Health. Filmed by Women's History Research Center	630
Woolf, Virginia Stephen. Orlando; MS From Knole Kent	631

Item No.

World Council of Churches. Commission on Faith and Order. Official Publications, 1910-1962	632
World Health Organization. World Health	633
World Treaty Index	363
Wright, Lyle H. American Fiction	13
The Writings of Daniel Defoe	146
The Writings of Thomas Jefferson With a Comprehensive Analytical Index	334
Yoruba Mission; Niger Mission; South African Mission; East African Mission; Nyanza Mission; Kenya Mission. Committee Records	118
Zarlino, Gioseffo. De tutte l'opere del R. M. Gioseffo Zarlino da Chioggia	634

Ref
Z
6620
C2
W33